the
Brainy
Bunch

The Harding Family's Method to College Ready by Age Twelve

the Brainy Bunch

Kip and Mona Lisa Harding

Gallery Books

New York   London   Toronto   Sydney   New Delhi

Gallery Books
An Imprint of Simon & Schuster, Inc.
1230 Avenue of the Americas
New York, NY 10020

First Gallery Books trade paperback edition September 2020

GALLERY BOOKS and colophon are registered trademarks of Simon & Schuster, Inc.

For information about special discounts for bulk purchases, please contact Simon & Schuster Special Sales at 1-866-506-1949 or business@simonandschuster.com.

The Simon & Schuster Speakers Bureau can bring authors to your live event. For more information or to book an event, contact the Simon & Schuster Speakers Bureau at 1-866-248-3049 or visit our website at www.simonspeakers.com.

Interior design by Akasha Archer
Cover photo © Morgan E. Jones

Manufactured in the United States of America

10 9 8 7 6 5 4 3 2 1

Library of Congress Cataloging-in-Publication Data is available.

ISBN 978-1-4767-5934-0
ISBN 978-1-4767-5935-7 (pbk)
ISBN 978-1-4767-5936-4 (ebook)

To Auntie Cilla, Aunt Mimi, and Cousin Maury,
for their expression of love and care for our family
and for being women among women.

Family Tree

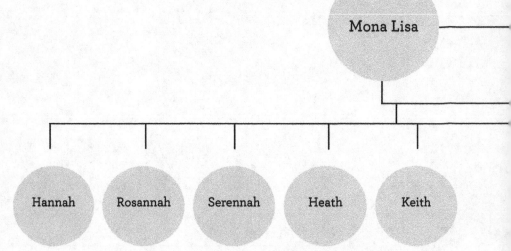

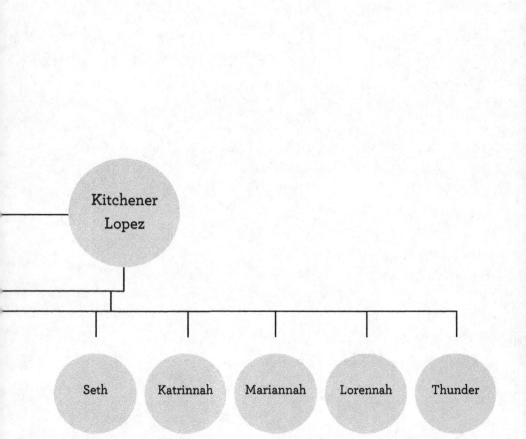

Contents

CONTENTS

Foreword

During the legal battles that I fought over twenty-five years ago to give parents the right to teach their own children in my state, one could not foresee the full array of advantages that homeschooling would provide. Alex and Brett Harris worked for me at the Alabama Supreme Court at age sixteen and wrote *Do Hard Things* out of that experience, challenging young people not to conform to the low expectations of society for their age group. Now the Hardings have demonstrated how the age threshold can be pushed back even further by the individualized tailoring of educational opportunities afforded by devoted parents in their home. At a time when public education is in a constant state of crisis over poor results, this book is a must-read for loving, conscientious parents seeking the best for their children.

Justice Tom Parker
Alabama Supreme Court

Introduction

The Greenhouse Effect

Train up a child in the way he should go: and when he is old, he
will not depart from it.
—PROVERBS 22:6

This isn't a story about geniuses or driven parents obsessed with their children. We like to think this is a love story, about how an ordinary couple met in high school and were eventually blessed with an amazing set of children. It's a story of faith, and how that faith defined how we chose to parent. It's also a story about dreams, about instilling them into kids with average intelligence and allowing them to blossom. We thank God for our family and for inventing this wonderful thing called homeschooling. Our true hope is that you'll be inspired reading about all the possibilities homeschooling has to offer.

Before sharing with you who we are and how we got to this point, we want to start by talking about why we choose to homeschool. We realize there's a stigma attached to this word. But homeschooling has come a long way in the last couple of decades.

When we first started homeschooling in 1997, we did not have all of the online resources that we do now. We felt like we had to find the material for our kids and try to supply all of the answers that their little curious minds could come up with. Now when they have a question we can't answer, we say, "Wow, that is such a good question." Then we suggest they Google it and tell us since we really want to know the answer, too. They usually come back a few minutes later with so much interesting information. And even if we're not too interested in the subject matter, we are so thrilled to see that spark in their eyes that this newfound knowledge has put there.

Our kids teach us something every day and they are learning to find answers on their own. We do not have to worry about what they are missing in their education. We, as parents, just have to make sure that they have access to the Internet, good books, and our attention.

The amount of resources instantly available is remarkable. There are tools and techniques for homeschooling that we will share with you later in this book. But for now, we'd like to share the eleven primary reasons why we (and many other families—over 2 million kids as of 2013!) choose to homeschool (our source for the homeschooling statistics is www.topmastersineducation.com/homeschooled/):

1. There is a lot of "dumbing down" going on in the American school, as John Taylor Gatto explained in one of his books. Kids are not allowed to learn at their own pace in public and most private schools. Many kids get bored in school because the teacher has to teach to the middle of the class. He or she cannot move forward with the kids who are ready to move and doesn't have time to really help the kids who are falling behind.

2. There are places like Selma, Alabama, where 40 percent of students do not graduate from high school. The public school system is failing. If you have doubts, just watch the documentary *Waiting for "Superman."* As an early private school kid who later worked as a high school math and science teacher, our oldest daughter clearly saw how little learning actually goes on in a classroom of over twenty-plus kids as opposed to the quality of the education she got at home with personal attention.

3. We believe in a Christian worldview and creation. We believe that there is scientific evidence that supports intelligent design. Uncle Sam will pay for kids to learn only a single theory, which limits diversity of opinion and growth.

4. Our right to pray in school is being challenged everywhere (and has already been taken away in many places) even though it is still our constitutional right. Thirty-six percent of homeschooling families say that providing religion to their children is their first concern.

5. We believe teaching kids in an age-segregated environment is not the most effective way to develop real-life social skills and exposes them to peer pressure. It is not the way the real world works. In the real world, we encounter people of all different ages. We want to teach our kids how to interact with people of all ages. Homeschooled kids are less peer-dependent and better socially adjusted for the real world.

6. We were both educated in the public school system and we know all about how much time is wasted sitting around, standing in line, and excessively practicing concepts. Our daughter had to ride the bus for forty-five minutes each way to and from the private school that she attended for her first four years of school. At home, we can be done with our school day by lunch and have time in the afternoon to read more books for pleasure, to play, to go on field trips, or to have bonding time with the family. No homework for Dad to deal with when he gets home.

7. We do not have to worry about school shootings or any other kind of school bullying and violence, which has recently been in the media so much and is scary for all parents.

8. Now that we have kids graduating from college at the ages of seventeen and fifteen, we can't turn back. Not even a private school setting could give us the results that we are getting—results that our children have worked hard for and desire themselves.

9. We are free to tailor our curriculum to match the interests of each child. For example, we can study one subject in depth and with great continuity, teaching how it may relate to other subjects. Kids really learn better when they can see the big picture of how each subject integrates with the others.

> HOMESCHOOLING WORKS. ON AVERAGE, HOMESCHOOLERS SCORE IN THE EIGHTY-SEVENTH PERCENTILE ON STANDARDIZED TESTS.

10. Homeschooling works. On average, homeschoolers score in the eighty-seventh percentile on standardized tests. Seventy-four percent of homeschoolers continue on to college, as opposed to 49 percent of the general population. Ninety-nine percent have read a book in the last six months, as opposed to only 69 percent of everyone else. And as you'll see from our story, you can achieve amazing things through homeschooling.

11. You cannot pay for a better education outside of your home. Homeschoolers on average spend $500 per child per year, whereas the average public school spends almost $10,000—for worse results.

What is the greenhouse effect? Think of your home as a greenhouse where your new little seedlings can begin to take root and grow into big strong plants. Once your plants are mature enough to be transplanted outside to face the elements, you will be able to take them out of the greenhouse. We use this precious time before our "little plants" start college to teach them all we can about the outside world.

Kids have so many questions, questions like "Where do babies come from?" The answer you give your five-year-old is so different from the answer you give your ten-year-old. This will open up discussions about biology, psychology, and sociology. Why would you want them to get their answer from a textbook and an overworked and underpaid schoolteacher who really doesn't know your child? Or, even worse, what if they get the answer from another child on the playground like many of us did?

It's a beautiful thing when we're able to be the ones there to give our children the best answers. And not only the best answers, but the love and bonding that comes in providing those answers.

This book is the story of our journey into homeschooling and how we managed to achieve the success we've had with our children. Our desire is not for others to imitate us but rather for them to be encouraged. We want others to follow their dreams and know that attending college early may be an option.

For our family, attending college early is the best option we know. And it really is something that can be achieved with hard work, perseverance, and faith.

A recent report (www.educationnews.org/parenting/number-of-homeschoolers-growing-nationwide/) in *Education News* states that since 1999, the number of children who are homeschooled has increased by 75 percent. Though homeschooled children represent only 4 percent of all school-age children nationwide, the number of children whose parents choose to educate them at home rather than in a traditional academic setting is growing seven times faster than the number of children enrolling in grades K–12 every year.

Source: http://www.breitbart.com/Big-Government/2013/06/07/
Report-Growth-in-Homeschooling-Outpacing-Public-Schools

· · · · · · ·

There is no school equal to a decent home,
and no teacher equal to a virtuous parent.
—MAHATMA GANDHI

1

Meet the Brainy Bunch

Let the words of my mouth, and the meditation of my heart, be
acceptable in thy sight, O Lord, my strength, and my redeemer.
—PSALM 19:14

I f you called the Harding house, an appropriate greeting message
might sound something like this:

Hi, you have reached the Hardings.
If you are looking for an engineering consultant, press 1.
If you need architectural advice, press 2.
If you need medical advice, press 3.
For the computer help desk, press 4.
If you need someone to play violin at your daughter's wedding, press 5.
If you want to learn the truth about the Viking horned helmet, press 6.
If you need legal advice from a ten-year-old's perspective, press 7.
If you need help finding your car keys, cell phone, or any other lost
   item, press 8.

If you want to hear poetic readings of Dr. Seuss, press 9.
If you are looking for a wrestling partner, press 1, then 0.
If you would like to make a donation to the Harding College Fund
   or talk to Kip or Mona Lisa, please leave a message at the beep.

We would love to tell you that we are geniuses and that our children have our special, unique DNA to match our brilliance. Yet this is hardly the case. We are your average family and your average neighbors with ten children. Well, okay, maybe that is not so average. But if you have met some big homeschooling families, you might already have some preconceived ideas of what we are about. Like the list of reasons why we homeschool, we thought we'd share what the Brainy Bunch really looks like.

First off, we are Christians. We love our Lord Jesus with all our hearts and have dedicated our lives to teaching our children to love Jesus first and others second. If we succeed in this, then we have fulfilled our purpose on this earth.

Second, we are not perfect. We fail all the time. We fight just like everybody else. We yell at each other in anger at times, yet we know how to forgive. We try really hard to forgive as we have been forgiven.

Third, as we said, we are *not* geniuses. Every member of our family is of average intelligence. There is nothing special about our genes. Our kids have been able to start college by the age of twelve because of two things: the grace of God and the vision to accelerate our teaching methods that we have come to through Him.

The fourth thing you should know about us is that we are not experts. We continue to figure out things as we go. We did different things with our first daughter than what we are doing now with our youngest children. We cannot tell people, "Do this list of things and your child will be ready to enter college by age twelve." However, we do have a general method that we have been following and we have gotten pretty nice results considering who our children are (more on them very shortly).

The fifth and final thing about us is that we want to help others. We feel called to write things down and speak to others on the matter of homeschooling. In light of Deuteronomy 6:6–7, we feel that Christians do best to keep their kids with them as much as possible. It's such a privilege and an honor to be given children on this earth. We do not feel that strangers should educate our children. If you have children, they are on loan to you for a short time. Do not miss out and send them away for seven to eight hours a day, not even to a Christian school, while they are so young.

That's a strong statement but we stand behind it. We are well informed in our area and feel that as Christians it is our God-given responsibility to keep our children home while they are young and impressionable. We understand that single parents will need outside help if they feel the same calling.

Have we always felt this way? Not at all. We grew into this belief, as you'll come to find out. For a while, our eldest daughters went to a private school. Although I (Mona Lisa) wanted to homeschool from the beginning, I gave in to the pressure of doing what all the other parents were doing. It was only after Hannah (our eldest) finished third grade and Kip reentered active duty in the air force that I realized I wouldn't have to work anymore and could start what I should have done in the first place.

We were learning back then and we continue to learn now.

Our story began out of broken families. Kip grew up in a home weighed down by divorce, yet God still reached down and saved him in the seventh grade. I (Mona Lisa) grew up in a home crippled by the death of my father, but God reached down and saved me in my late teens. I was living in San Jose, California, when Kip asked me to prom. A few weeks after that, he proposed to me.

I took Natural Family Planning (NFP) classes to prepare to be a good Catholic wife. I knew that this was the only form of birth control that the Catholic Church endorsed and I was trying to be a *good* Catholic. To be honest, I was afraid of having a dozen kids. It's funny that this is exactly what I'm praying for now—twelve children to love and teach.

My mother was an "old-school" Catholic who didn't think I should be learning NFP at all because she believed that truly good Catholics, especially Hispanics, should have *all* the kids that God wants to give them. Just like her mother did. My faith wasn't there yet. I wanted to make sure this NFP stuff really worked. So after waiting one month and having one fertile cycle with no pregnancy, I was ready to have a baby! So voilà! Hannah was conceived when we were both eighteen.

Looking back, I remember how we had such a childlike faith. We didn't know much about raising a baby, but we trusted that God would take care of us.

He always has.

Not only that, but He's given us ten incredible reasons to thank Him daily.

Hannah is now twenty-five years old. She was the trailblazer (or some would say guinea pig!) in our family. She was gifted in math and was brave enough to try her first online college algebra math class at the age of twelve. She did this at Cuesta College while dual-enrolled in homeschooling. She then completed the California High School Proficiency Exam (CHSPE) the next semester and took two more classes at Allan Hancock College in the summer of 2001. Hannah was full-time in college at age thirteen and played soccer for the women's team.

One of the best things about Hannah was her fearlessness. She wasn't afraid of failure because she had the love and support of her family. She earned a BS in mathematics by age seventeen from Auburn University at Montgomery (AUM). She went on to earn two master's degrees, in math and engineering, at Cal State East Bay in Hayward, California, and Tuskegee University in Alabama. She loves learning and is returning to Tuskegee University this fall to work on a PhD in engineering on a full scholarship.

Our second-born is **Rosannah**, who is twenty-three years old and the youngest architect in the American Institute of Architects (AIA). She has always been very independent and traveled abroad to Mexico City, where she met her husband, Sergio, a fellow architect from Peru. She completed a five-year architecture program at the age of eighteen at California College of the Arts and was married at nineteen. She worked for a firm in San Francisco before moving to New York City in August 2013 to attend the famed Cooper Union on a full college scholarship for an MS in architecture.

SERENNAH IS TWENTY-TWO AND ONE OF THE YOUNGEST FEMALE DOCTORS IN THE NAVY AND IN THE U.S.

Rosannah has been privileged to be on an architecture team that designed a medical school for women in Saudi Arabia. She was also on an award-winning architecture team that designed the second-largest border crossing from Mexico into the United States.

Serennah is twenty-two and one of the youngest female doctors in the navy and in the U.S. At the age of ten or eleven, she felt called by God to be a physician. She took the SAT at age eleven and started part-time at AUM. She then transferred for two years to Santa Clara University in the San Francisco Bay Area. Moving once again as a military dependent, she transferred to Huntingdon College and graduated with a BA degree in biology at seventeen. She is now stationed as a navy doctor in Bethesda, Maryland, and doing her residency. She may ship out soon.

Our first son is **Heath**, who is seventeen and has completed an MS in computer science. From the time he was four he learned more on his own than from direct parental instruction, with the help of his big sisters as homeschool companions. He actually started his first college class while dual-enrolled at age ten at Foothill College, in Los Altos, California. He eventually passed all areas of the CHSPE. He then transferred to AUM in the summer of 2007 and studied part-time. That fall he attended Huntingdon and was enrolled there full-time by age eleven. He earned a BS in English at the age of fifteen.

In addition to his two part-time jobs, Heath is has founded a new business that will launch as AbstractEducation.com. They will be selling web-based abstracts and condensed learning materials for a variety of college-level courses.

Keith is fifteen and a college senior at Faulkner University. He started college by age eleven and chose mostly music theory and performance classes. Although he is the quiet and shy type, we are amazed at how he enjoys playing the piano, clarinet, and violin and singing in front of large crowds. He also was voted president of the choir at his college and has been honored as a section leader playing the clarinet in the band. His appreciation for classical music and the talent he shows is quite extraordinary and is a testament to the quality of instruction he has received while at Faulkner University.

Seth is twelve and started studying history at Faulkner University at the age of eleven. He still acts like a typical twelve-year-old boy but academically thrives in his college-level courses—he had the highest average in his history class! He is transferring to Huntingdon College this fall. He loves the Middle Ages/Dark Ages and is an enthusiast of the art of medieval combat and all things to do with knights, medieval customs, Vikings, and the archaeology of those periods of history.

Katrinnah is ten and took the ACT in April of 2013. She has a bubbly personality and would like to get onto a stage very soon. She likes to sing and dance and dress up in fabulous-looking outfits. She also has an interest in law and defending some of our American freedoms. We are tailoring her high school curriculum to match her interests and are considering a combination of prelaw and acting for her undergraduate work.

Mariannah is eight and is working on becoming an independent reader. She talks of becoming a doctor like big sister Serennah. She is very kind and gentle with her younger siblings and is very careful with helping to meet their needs. She was baptized at our local church in June of 2013 and is learning dance as part of her homeschooling.

Lorennah is five and spends most of her time practicing writing her letters and playing with her little brother, Thunder. She likes all things pink and related to princesses. She is a real joy in our home and is affectionately called Lori-B, our Southern belle.

Finally, there is **Thunder**, a very opinionated three-year-old who believes that he is a Superman/Spider-Man combo. His name is based on an actual event, when lightning struck a large oak in our backyard and blew out five windows in our home. Nine months later to the day, he was born. He shows early signs of athleticism, and we wonder what God has in store for this one.

These are the ten gifts God has given us. Each one is unique and exceptional in his or her own way. We love each one dearly and are amazed to watch them learn and grow. They are all special, yet at the same time they are ordinary children. They are girls and boys who have shown that homeschooling techniques like the ones we'll be talking about with you do in fact work. If you meet them you'll discover they're just like other kids their age. Yet they are also blessed to have parents who want them to dream and want to encourage them in every way with those dreams.

This homeschooling adventure has been quite the journey, as you'll come to read in what our children have written. But speaking of dreams, it's been our dream that God keeps making come true. We hope it will be the same for you.

From the Kids

My Encouraging Homeschooling Story
by Hannah Harding (written at age 19)
[2007]

As I get ready for graduation from California State University (East Bay), many memories of the struggles that my parents went through to educate me come to mind. One of these took place when I was only four years old in our little house in rural Kansas. My father was taking a business calculus class, and he wanted to teach me how to compute the derivative. He simply showed me how to move the exponent down in front of the variable and then subtract the exponent by one and so on. At first, I did some wrong and got frustrated, but after a few tries I did one right. My father praised me for this accomplishment. I got really excited because I felt that I had just done something really good, whatever it was. Of course, I did not actually know what a derivative was at the time, but I understood how to move numbers around and subtract them.

Throughout my life, my father has continued to encourage me to do great things even if I did not think I could at first. As I look back, I think of how I would have never made it to where I am today if it were not for my parents' involvement in my education. They decided to teach me at home when I was just an average third grader in a private school. Their decision was not only for financial reasons, but for our well-being and our future.

My parents have had to deal with a lot of criticism from people who have never heard of homeschooling. They would ask questions like, "What about socialization?" as if we would never come into contact with other human beings if we were homeschooled. This was ridiculous, of course. Besides being part of a big family, we interacted with many other homeschoolers through chess clubs, sports activities, art days, church events, soccer teams, and neighborhood children.

Many people choose to home-educate their kids for various reasons. My parents did it because of religious reasons and because they could see the higher quality in the behavior and intellect of children who were homeschooled compared to those who were not. People would ask if my parents had teaching credentials, to which I would respond, "No, and it is not necessary." This is not to say that my parents were not educated but that they did not major in education. My father is now working on a doctorate in education. Since I already knew how to read and write, I simply read books about many subjects and did a lesson in math every day. My mother did most of my homeschooling, which consisted mainly of answering math questions if I could not find the answer in the solutions manual. I found that this was the best method for me to learn. After all, many famous mathematicians were self-taught, including Blaise Pascal.

For English, I would write essays on many topics or I would write in my journal and my mom would correct my spelling and grammar. My dad was the one who encouraged me to start doing two lessons of math every day, because he believed that once I became proficient in mathematics, that was the doorway to success. He was right. By the age of twelve, my parents knew that I was more advanced in math than they were. However, they did not view this as a problem, but merely an obstacle to overcome. Therefore, my parents decided to let me take an online math class at a community college as a high school student.

After that semester, I took the California High School Proficiency Exam (CHSPE), which is the equivalent of a high school diploma. In order to take this exam, a person has to be fifteen or in the second semester of their sophomore year. My parents knew that I was doing sophomore-level work, so I took the test. I had to show the test proctor my military ID (identification card), since I did not have a driver's license. Military kids everywhere are eligible to get an ID at age ten. This was great since I needed it to take the ACT/SAT. My mother called this "getting in through the back door." No one knew how old I was, and I did not tell them. I passed at the age of thirteen. At first I cried from being overwhelmed by the thought of enrolling during the summer as a full-time student on a real college campus. Then, my father and mother explained that it would only be part-time. My mother assured me that she would be nearby walking with my siblings around the college track for exercise. They made me realize my newfound freedom: I felt that I could accomplish anything I set my mind to. That summer I took two classes and played soccer for college credit because I loved to play the game. By the fall, I was accepted onto the women's collegiate soccer team and started in every game.

Another thing people think about my parents' homeschooling is that they pushed me too hard, but I never felt that way. On one occasion, my father found out the night before a test that I had not studied for it. My reasoning was that because I did well on all of the homework throughout the course, I did not need to review it or practice. Basically, though, I was lazy and I sometimes struggle with this today. I felt guilty because that weekend before the test I had been playing soccer and spending time with some old friends who had come from out of town, and

I neglected to study. After receiving a thorough lecture from my father, I started crying. He rubbed my back and just explained how it didn't matter and how he still loved me. He told me that all he expected of me is that I do my best work, and that is all I could do. At that moment, I realized that I was not really prepared for my test because I had not done my best work. He said, "If being a full-time student and playing on the soccer team is too much, you can be a part-time student the next semester. You are only fourteen and you are way ahead of your peers. You have plenty of time." I was greatly encouraged and began to improve my study methods. I got a B in that precalculus class and A's in all the others. The real lesson that I took away from this experience is how important it is that I always do my best work.

I have continued as a full-time student every semester since then and graduated magna cum laude in 2005 and I am graduating spring 2007 from California State University (East Bay) with my MS in mathematics. I write about myself not to brag but to testify to the truth of my parents' accomplishments. Their decision to teach me at home, without question, has had a profound impact on my life. My parents were not discouraged by the criticisms of others and showed me my potential that I could not see on my own. If it were not for their wise decision, I would be like every other high school kid.

Furthermore, I have made the decision that I will do the same for my children someday, regardless of opposition from others. From my point of view, I have to look no further than my own siblings for encouraging success stories of homeschoolers. My seventeen-year-old sister is in her fifth year of the architecture program at California College of the Arts (GPA. 3.8, higher than mine). She hopes to own a firm someday and wants to design residential buildings. My other sister, now age sixteen, is majoring in premed biology at Santa Clara University and desires to be a doctor. My eleven-year-old brother has dreams of becoming an actor/director/producer and is taking drama classes. He is right on my tail, mathematically speaking, because he has completed intermediate algebra and is taking statistics.

My other siblings are still very young, but I know that they will accomplish much more than I did at their age, since they have been homeschooled from the beginning. Now, as I look at my degree, I think of all the struggles that my parents went through to help me get here. When I look back on my life and its humble beginnings, I begin to question why I am so blessed. A verse in Jeremiah 29:11 comes to mind: "For I know the plans that I have for you, declares the Lord, plans for welfare and not for calamity to give you a future and a hope." I am sure that God's derivation of His plan for my life is far better than anything that I could calculate or my parents could encourage.

2

How Did You Do It?

When he was twelve years old, they went up to the festival,
according to the custom. After the festival was over, while his
parents were returning home, the boy Jesus stayed behind in
Jerusalem, but they were unaware of it. Thinking he was in their
company, they traveled on for a day. Then they began looking for
him among their relatives and friends. When they did not find him,
they went back to Jerusalem to look for him. After three days they
found him in the temple courts, sitting among the teachers, listening
to them and asking them questions. Everyone who heard him was
amazed at his understanding and his answers.

—LUKE 2:42–47

Twelve is a special number, a perfect number in the Bible. Think about it. There were twelve patriarchs, twelve sons of Israel, and twelve disciples chosen. So it's no surprise that in scripture we read that Mary and Joseph found Jesus in the temple at the age of twelve talking to the leaders. Hmm . . . maybe there *is* something special that happens around the age of twelve.

We have found that our children can reason, can think critically, can handle abstract ideas, and are ready for higher learning around this age. We've found that around the age of twelve, some kids get bored with school. I talk to moms all the time who are trying to motivate their kids to do their schoolwork. This is where Kip and I advise parents to find what really motivates their child. If they have an idea of what they want to do in life, then the parents can help tailor their education to what excites them. We found that our kids were ready to move on to bigger and better things around this age. Once they started college classes, I no longer had to motivate them to do their homework and study. Will all of our children be the same? I hope so. I can't be totally sure, but now we have a "target" age. It's a goal to shoot for. We just work hard every day and watch to see what their calling is.

> WE'VE FOUND THAT AROUND THE AGE OF TWELVE, SOME KIDS GET BORED WITH SCHOOL.

"So how did you do it?"

This is the common question that my husband and I get whenever we tell people about our kids. So I'll start out with *why* we decided to do it.

When Hannah, our oldest, was four, Kip would try to entertain her by teaching her how to "differentiate equations."

He was learning this procedure of calculus at the time and turned it into a game to keep her busy. It was a lot of fun bonding in this way because he could tell people, "Hey, look what Hannah can do!" She got a lot of attention from her dad by hanging out with him and taking an interest in math. Does this mean she was a genius at four?

No. She just blossomed because of the individual attention she was getting, and she grew to love math.

During this time period when Kip was working with Hannah to keep her entertained as he studied, I was working the evening shift in a nursing home. I met a night-shift nurse who homeschooled her five children. She would work nights, go home in the morning, get her kids up, and get them started on their chores, breakfast, and lessons. Her five kids (looking back, that seemed like a lot to me at the time!) were older and independent readers. She would go to bed after her husband left for work. After sleeping, she would wake up to correct schoolwork and make supper. Then there would be family time. I was amazed that she was managing a full-time job and homeschooling her kids. Watching her commitment made me very motivated to take on the responsibility of educating my children myself. I asked myself the following questions:

"Who loves my kids more than I do?"

"Who knows them better than I do?"

One of the reasons this nurse began homeschooling was that her son was labeled as having attention deficit disorder (ADD). She found out later that he was actually only misbehaving because he was bored. His schoolwork was not challenging enough, so he would finish quickly and then spend time fooling around in class. I have heard this scenario repeated in many other cases. (We won't address the issue of ADD in this book except to say that many a child has been mislabeled by professional educators only to completely excel when brought home to be educated.) Again, this may not always be the case, but many times it is. Even though my friend had this additional obstacle in educating her unique son, she still achieved great success. This special child was the catalyst that made her bring all of her children home.

Another friend of mine with seven children also made the important decision to homeschool. The more I talked about homeschooling around her, the more convinced she became that it was a great idea. She decided to bring her younger children home because she was upset about the material her children were learning. Through her experience, I was able to see up close the planning and all the details of learning how to teach one's own children.

So even though I knew I wanted to do it, and I had friends who had inspired me and who could surely give me pointers along the way, I chickened out and gave in to self-doubt when it came time for Hannah to go to school, convincing myself I wasn't up for it. I decided to enroll her in a private school for kindergarten. The Christian school I enrolled her in was supported by the church, so there was no tuition. Money was one of the determining factors. It was free for us and allowed me to be able to do day care in my home without having to learn to homeschool for a few more years. I kept Rosannah, Serennah, and Heath at home with me along with a few other local children. I also worked my nursing job on the weekends.

To this day Hannah jokingly tries to make us feel guilty for "sticking" her in school and "industrializing" her. She feels that she was "dumbed down" and could have excelled more at home. Considering she completed her bachelor's at seventeen, she was not slowed down too much! But she does regret the time that she spent away from her family. I really did miss her those first four years of school.

Now, just to make it clear, I do not feel negatively toward any of the teachers my girls had. But I do need to write about Rosannah's teacher to discuss a point. While my daughter was in the first and second grades, she received comments on her report cards indicating she was a "dreamer." I found out later that as a homeschooled child she did daydream a bit and liked to doodle. Many times she was drawing in her math notebook and in the margins of her notes instead of doing her work. My husband and I recognized when she was very young that she had true artistic ability. As far as being a dreamer, she was just being observant of her surroundings. While the rest of us are moving on to something else, she is in the back soaking it all in. She takes her time looking at things. She has been able to pick out interesting things about what she sees like no one else can. But in public school this was considered a drawback. Funny that she should grow up to study architecture, where doodling is a way of life and should be encouraged!

Too many children lose their passion for learning when they are stuck in a public school setting. They get bored and spend too much time trying to concentrate on things that do not interest them. It's like going into a clothing store where one size fits all. In homeschooling, the education is tailor-made for the child's gifts and interests. I believe my daughter's dreams could have been squelched if she had gone to public school. Rosannah is thriving now and has accomplished so much, but what would have happened if she had stopped dreaming? Where would she have gone if she stopped observing and doodling? If she had conformed to what the teachers wanted her to do?

> ROSANNAH IS THRIVING NOW AND HAS ACCOMPLISHED SO MUCH, BUT WHAT WOULD HAVE HAPPENED IF SHE HAD STOPPED DREAMING?

I am saddened when I see kids being held back in high school by taking four years to finish. I feel that if the parents would allow them, they could do so much more. It is even sadder to see homeschool parents attempting to mimic public school curriculums. Then when it understandably becomes too demanding for the parent, or too boring for the child, they take that as a sign to send them back to the hired help (public or private educators).

When Hannah was barely five years old we bought some kindergarten workbooks and started working with her in the mornings. My husband, Kip, would do his college homework in the afternoons and evenings and keep her occupied by teaching her those complex math concepts. It is interesting since she finished her master's in mathematics and is working toward a PhD. He did not choose this field of study for her at age four, she was just wired for math by God, just like Rosannah was given the gift of creativity and design, which is so evident as she is doing so well as an architect.

Homeschooling doesn't take parents with any particular advanced education, just a heart for their child and a willingness to want their child to go far. Our third daughter, Serennah, has an extremely wise and compassionate heart and always wanted to help others by becoming a physician. Her younger brother Heath was born when she was four and a half (our longest gap between kids), so she was quite the little mommy. She also helped me a lot at that age while I did child care at my home for a couple of babies in the area.

I can look back now and see how our girls' character traits have helped them develop certain skills. God worked out the details and somehow helped us to nurture the gifts with which our children were born.

As mentioned, we ended up sending our girls to a private school for a couple of years. I was working my nursing job on weekends (twelve-hour shifts) and doing day care in my home Monday through Friday. Because county workers had to monitor my home day care, I guess I did not want to answer a bunch of questions about why my kids were not in school.

But after Hannah finished the third grade, Kip reentered active duty in the air force and told me I would not have to work anymore. I look back now and realize that I was just afraid, as many mothers are. My convictions were not as strong as they are now. If I had to do it all over again, I would definitely try to balance working with homeschooling. With our older children reaching adulthood, we have additional help. There's always a way to work it all out. There are other families out there homeschooling even though the mom has to work. Some have grandparents helping out, some do shift work, many work from home, some have older kids who can be trusted to do the work independently, and some even take the kids to work with them whenever possible. I know now that if parents feel led to homeschool, they can pray about it and find a workable solution.

Our decision had been made, and we were fortunate to be able to finally take the homeschooling plunge.

Now the fun was about to begin.

From the Kids

Shooting for the Stars
by Rosannah Harding (written at age 22)
[2011]

I was blessed at an early age to know what I wanted to do with my life: to become an architect. I was also blessed with parents who encouraged me to pursue it and showed me that it was not that far from my reach.

I remember the moment I realized that I wanted to be an architect. Since early childhood, I paid attention to my surroundings and was much more interested in the way the light felt through the window than staring at a chalkboard. But even so, I had an appreciation for math in terms of its physical nature. The point where art and science collide seemed a perfect fit for me. There was something about the notion of creating something from nothing—or rather creating something from a single idea. I was so excited about the possibility that something in my mind's eye could become a reality.

In the early 2000s when the housing market was booming, my dad made a hobby of checking out model homes of new housing developments in central California. I would tag along and be amazed at the size and the scale of the spaces. As we were leaving the homes, I remember asking my mom, "Who is the person who decides where the rooms go?" She answered, "That would be an architect." That was it. When I discovered that it was an actual job—getting to make beautiful drawings for a living and envision spaces that get built into realities—I knew that was my calling.

I must have been ten years old at the time. It's amazing how

God plants a seed in our hearts, and it grows into a dream and you know without a doubt it is what you are meant to do.

For most parents out there, when their eight-year-old says to them, "I want to be an astronaut (or whatever profession it might be) when I grow up," they smile at their kid and say, "Oh, that's nice," and go about their day. My dad, on the other hand, would take it to heart. He would sign them up for the next Space Camp and introduce them to a friend of a friend who cleans rockets. My parents would do everything possible to show that the dream could be a reality.

Something that still resonates with me is the way my dad always encouraged us to set our goals and aim as high as we could. Don't just settle for the middle. "Shoot for the stars," he would say, "and maybe you'll land on the moon." I always took this to mean that if you aimed as high as you could and didn't make it there, you still might end up somewhere pretty amazing. But if you set your sights too low, you may never reach your potential.

To this day, this mind-set still drives me. Someday I want to open my own architectural firm with my husband and maybe friends from college. Why be a draftsperson when you can be your own boss and make your own designs a reality?

Mom and Dad did not regard age as an excuse for immaturity. They gave us responsibilities to help us grow and taught us to reason like adults. Because we were treated like adults—and by this I mean with the expectation that we were capable of a higher level of accountability—we often rose to the occasion and surpassed what would be considered the "norm" for our age. I think in many ways this prepared us for real-world decision making and gave us the confidence to participate with students several years our senior.

People always say to my siblings and me that we are so mature for our age. I think this all goes back to building those invaluable skills of communication and measuring consequences. Parents are ultimately raising adults, independent human beings who are capable of living and being a light in this world.

3

Motivated for More

Whatever your hand finds to do, do it with all your might, for in the realm of the dead, where you are going, there is neither working nor planning nor knowledge nor wisdom.
—ECCLESIASTES 9:10

We didn't wake up one morning and say, "Let's home-school our ten children!" Obviously life doesn't work out that way. God doesn't give you a big family right away. And just like the small number in our family, we started slowly with small goals and dreams.

The friend of ours with the seven kids who started homeschooling before I did advised me to begin with workbooks because I told her I needed to start in the easiest fashion possible. Personally, if something seems too complicated for me, I'd rather just not do it. This was an easy way to start. It's easy to get overwhelmed and just say "forget it." Many parents end up doing that. I knew this would be manageable if it was all laid out for me like the map to a buried treasure or a blueprint to a beautiful building.

As soon as school was out for the girls in May 1997, we traveled to Chico, California. I immediately ordered workbooks for their grade levels from Christian Light Publications. Hannah was starting fourth grade, Rosannah was starting third grade, and Serennah was starting first grade. I knew I wanted to do homeschooling in the beginning of the summer and teach all year-round.

While I am convinced homeschooling is an exceptional avenue in educating one's child, it is equally dependent on a Christian faith and curriculum for lifetime success. Without the faith ingredient, your child may be as smart as they come but still be as unwise, foolish, and possibly evil as can be.

I ordered the Alpha Omega (AOP.com) workbooks for each girl according to her grade level, and they studied the Bible, math, language arts, history, science, and Spanish. I quickly found out that it was easier to read biographies to my girls out loud because I enjoyed learning too. Somehow, I couldn't remember some of these interesting historical figures. It seems that in my public school education, many interesting people were introduced, but there was not enough time to really cover their lives in detail. However, at home we were able to pick the biographies that interested us. I learned so much and realized that I love history!

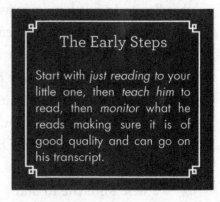

The Early Steps

Start with *just reading* to your little one, then *teach him* to read, then *monitor* what he reads making sure it is of good quality and can go on his transcript.

There are so many books that are written from a Christian worldview. I have plenty of material that I have collected over the years, some of which we've listed in the "Resources" section at the end of this book. One can't get that perspective from a public school education. From all the Christian material available, I was able to teach life truths. It was wonderful to discuss our values as we read the material.

As soon as the girls became good independent readers, they were free to choose what historical fiction books and biographies they wanted to read. Homeschooling at this juncture became monumentally easier. They quickly went from books written for children to unabridged versions of books. The more they read, the fewer grammar workbooks and spelling tests we did. I once read that kids learn grammar from reading. That was definitely true for my kids. As they continued to read more, their writing improved. We watched very little TV at this time, but we did rent a lot of educational videos from the library. We also enjoyed movies that are based on true stories that have an object lesson. My friend advised me to make them write every day. They started out writing letters to friends since we had recently moved from Kansas to California. Our girls also kept journals as an assignment.

If they were ever at a loss for words, they would copy a passage from the biblical book of Proverbs and have to paraphrase the meaning. There is a lot of wisdom in the book of Proverbs. I also once read that Benjamin Franklin improved his writing by copying essays that were written by others and then rewrote them and tried to improve them. So, when our children are around four years old, we let them start copying words from their favorite early readers. If they want to write a letter or an entry in their journal, they dictate to me and then they copy it on a separate sheet. In the middle grades, we use grammar books like *Editor in Chief* because they are a quick, concise way to teach rules and then get back to writing.

We were fortunate to find a nice homeschool group on the military base we moved to. Our girls were very motivated to get their schoolwork done so they could go outside to play. They became very efficient. Sometimes they would do their math lessons the night before in order to be ahead the next day. They did this on their own initiative.

After seeing our daughters' progress, Kip decided to double up on the math lessons because the reality is that the SAT standardized test gives two scores, one for verbal and one for math. We really began to emphasize those two areas. Their reading was focused on science and history, depending on their interests. One daughter liked creation science instead of evolution books. Another daughter liked to read about anatomy, physiology, and medicine.

When summer came along, I would always find it easier to have some structure by doing school all year-round. I remembered how I was bored at times during the summers when I was younger. And sometimes kids have too much unsupervised time on their hands. You will rarely hear my kids say they are bored! They only get that way when Mom and Dad mix up their own priorities and put their children last.

Even though we did schoolwork the whole year, the school days were much shorter than a public school day. So, in the end, our kids have had more time to pursue their interests and have fun. The other benefit is that there is no need to spend a month reviewing at the beginning of a new school year like I had to do in public school. This way our kids get through grade levels much quicker and with less effort, still having plenty of time to play and use their imagination.

Limiting television really helps their creativity. But we encourage them to watch intelligent programming. We just take the time to watch things with them and see if they're wholesome or not.

I remember trying to re-create school at home during these early years. Most new homeschoolers do this. Some even buy individual desks for each child. I felt like we had to "do school" all day Monday through Friday from eight A.M. to three P.M. It was a struggle waking the girls up early enough to do their chores in order to start school by eight A.M. I felt compelled to hit every subject every day, just like

I had to in school. It was exhausting for me and them, and the kids weren't learning any better.

After a few months of simply trying to re-create school at home, we wanted to do things our own way. We started to realize that we could have so much more fun if we (Mom included) could just study what we wanted. None of us were really enjoying all of the grammar exercises. We started to just journal every day and revise as we went along. We started to see lots of improvement in their writing and they were becoming good storytellers as they journaled. We knew that we were onto something. The girls were having fun by just reading and writing what they wanted.

Hannah resisted at first because she realized that Mom was a little too relaxed. There was a lot more structure at the school she had been previously attending. I guess this made her a little nervous. I remember Hannah saying to me, "Mrs. Miller [her former third-grade teacher] did not do it like that." This is when my eight-year-old had to get the "I am not Mrs. Miller" speech. Once Hannah saw that homeschooling was going to be different but better, she lightened up. She eventually poured herself into math and science. She did mathematics and read about mathematicians and scientists.

ONCE HANNAH SAW THAT HOMESCHOOLING WAS GOING TO BE DIFFERENT BUT BETTER, SHE LIGHTENED UP.

We know most educators believe that the more structure students have, the better the outcomes. We think quite differently. Studying for the ACT would come a few years later, but at this point it was just about learning how to become self-learners and enjoying every moment of being together at home studying what we enjoy together.

The other big change was that we realized there was so much learning going on in our daily lives that had nothing to do with actual "bookwork." Some have come to call this style of learning "unschooling." We define it as a relaxed way of learning as you go throughout your day. Anyone can adopt this attitude, even those who do not homeschool. We started to not worry so much about the questions at the end of every chapter. If we all agreed that there was real learning going on in the reading of the material, was it really necessary to answer all of those questions at the end? If the child wanted to, great. If the child wanted to move on to some other interesting reading material, that was okay, too.

I quickly threw out spelling tests and standardized testing and especially grammar. We tested the girls a couple of times and decided that we were not interested in testing them anymore. They did fine. It was expensive and was an unnecessary stress. We now focus on the two standardized tests that really matter, the ACT and the SAT.

We actually started having fun and the girls began to excel as they explored their own interests. If Mom wanted to skip the exercises and take a field trip, even better! It was on one of those field trips that Rosannah learned about architecture. And, likewise, it was on one of those field trips, to UCLA Medical Center, that Serennah got to sit in on several pre-op discussions. We insisted that she be able to listen in on those many visits because of her early interest in medicine. Kids everywhere could probably benefit from less bookwork and a few more real-life experiences.

So it started well. But the real test would come when the math became tougher.

Before I knew it, our oldest daughter reached my level of proficiency in mathematics. I had to hand her over to her father to help her with her homework. I had completed a year of trigonometry my senior year of high school and soon forgot most of what I had learned once I graduated. I was expecting our sixth child and was physically too

KIP AND MONA LISA HARDING

tired to relearn trigonometry. Kip took over tutoring her in math and a lightbulb went on in his head: he realized that she could be earning college credit for all of this higher-level math. This was about the same time as a homeschool conference we attended where we learned about the California High School Proficiency Exam (CHSPE) and met another family who had high school-age homeschoolers who were earning dual-enrollment credit at Cuesta College.

Seeing Hannah learn trigonometry with her father's help, and afterward in college, I realized that my children could become well educated regardless of whether or not I had a degree. Although I had been accepted to Santa Clara University when I was seventeen and could have earned my own degree, I had decided to marry my high school sweetheart and be a mom instead. (Yes, ladies, it is okay to "just" want to be a mom.) I never felt the need to pursue a college degree once I started down the path of marriage and family. After a few years, I did complete one year of nursing school to become a licensed practical nurse. This came about due to our financial need as Kip left his first tour of army active duty and was working toward his baccalaureate degree. I saw that I could double my income as a nurse's aide by completing just one year of school. I am slowly working on taking a couple of online courses toward an RN degree. It may take me several years to finish. Quite honestly, I am very content with my job of helping my kids pursue their own careers. I get a bigger thrill from having had my daughter Serennah attend Santa Clara University than if I had attended myself.

Perhaps this is a good place to discuss how we would feel if our daughters decided to become "stay-at-home" moms. We would love it! This, in our opinion, would be one of the most wonderful things they could do. We hope that someday all of our daughters and future daughters-in-law will be able to have my experience, because we have been so blessed by our children; they are a great source of joy. In the meantime, only God knows when and if they will all marry. So we support them now in their dreams of having careers.

I have several friends with college degrees who have chosen to become homeschooling moms. They have no regrets. Their parents or other family members have had negative things to say about how they are "wasting" their education. These moms know that it is not possible to "waste" an education when raising children. We will never say this to our daughters or daughters-in-law. My husband and I have an understanding that he will be the provider and I will be the keeper of the home. This works for us. My role as a wife and mother gives me a lot of joy and security. I put my trust in God to provide for us through my husband. I know this may not be a popular view, but it is a biblical one.

> IT IS NOT POSSIBLE TO "WASTE" AN EDUCATION WHEN RAISING CHILDREN.

We enrolled Hannah, at the age of twelve, in an online intermediate algebra course at Cuesta College in San Luis Obispo, California. She earned a B in this class. Around this time I went to a homeschool conference and met a fifteen-year-old who was taking college classes because she had passed the CHSPE. Do you see what good can come out of homeschool conferences? I recommend looking for any near you and attending. So, upon her example, in April of 2001, Hannah took the CHSPE and passed. The regulations stated that a student had to be age fifteen *or* a second-semester sophomore. This is a loophole to some educators but we think of it as a window of opportunity. When I sent in her application and received her admission letter shortly thereafter, there were no questions asked. I don't know if they even noticed that she was only thirteen. My guess is that they receive so many applications that maybe they don't check. Perhaps it was the same with the online class. No one made an issue of her age.

During the online class, I took Hannah to the actual classroom for three exams and the final. Picture this scene: a very pregnant woman sitting in a lawn chair outside the classroom while Hannah's younger siblings played on the lawn. This allowed her to feel that she was safe, since I was nearby, so she could concentrate on her academics.

When she took the CHSPE and passed, Kip and I were elated. Yet Hannah became very emotional and began to cry. We didn't understand why until she told us her fears. She was afraid that we were now going to enroll her in a full load of fourteen units and just drop her off at the campus and say, "See you later!" Once we convinced her that we would take it very slowly and we would be very sensitive to her needs, she was more at ease. She still needed her parents despite her amazing developments.

This was a valuable lesson to us and prompted us to start teaching our kids something very important: It's *okay* to pursue something that may be difficult if you are not afraid to fail. Sometimes the fear of failure keeps people from doing good things.

So Hannah took it slowly. The plan was for her to take one English class and one math class. I drove her to the campus, walked her to the classroom, and took my younger kids to the track. We walked around the track and met her in the car when the class was over. She felt secure and I felt good that I was not emotionally harming my child.

I received some criticism from some homeschooling friends about what we were doing, but my husband and I had a peace about this. Hannah did very well, earning a B in English and an A in her geometry class. The professors either did not notice that she was very young or chose not to point it out. She was treated like any other student and we liked it that way. We did not want her to get too much attention.

College can be the carrot to motivate a teenager who is getting bored with your level of homeschooling. Many parents have shared with us that they have had troubles motivating their teenagers to do their schoolwork. Sometimes students will work harder for a professor because they want to get that A. Getting A's at an early age in college is bound to attract attention. We certainly were not out to gain any special attention. But we have received a little of that on a few separate occasions with our other daughters.

Looking back, Hannah got some attention when she joined the women's soccer team. There was some media coverage. She was interviewed by two local TV stations and the local newspaper. She is very focused and humble so none of this went to her head. She kept working very hard and was self-motivated. In fact, we had to tell her to take a break, relax, and come sit and watch a movie with the family sometimes. She did not work so hard because we made her, but because she just wanted to do her best.

During this same time period, I was having trouble motivating our second daughter, Rosannah, to do her math. She would spend time doodling in her math book. It was very motivating for her when we told her that she was next in line to take the CHSPE at the age of twelve. We made studying the review book part of her curriculum. We reminded her that she had nothing to lose by attempting to pass this exam. If Rosannah did not pass, she could always take it again. This attitude has given our kids a lot of confidence. Unfortunately, she did not pass the first time. But because she was so close to passing and was doing eleventh-grade work, we decided to enroll her at Allan Hancock College in their College Now! program. She did well on their entrance exam and was pretty confident since her first class would be English 101 and she would be taking it with her older sister.

At this time we had an eighteen-year-old neighbor who was attending the same college and would drive our daughters back and forth to class. Rosannah did pass the CHSPE the second time around. She then moved up to two classes in the summer. I went back to walking around the track to be near the girls. In the fall, they started studying in the library together in between classes so they could be together. Most of their classmates just assumed that they were high school age. They only told people their age if they wanted to. There was some awkwardness when I would visit the financial aid and admissions offices to do paperwork when their ages came up. For the most part, people were just curious about how they got there so young. I shared with them about homeschooling and how they were able to graduate early, and most of the comments were very positive.

So there were already two college students in our house. Their ages were fourteen and twelve.

....

There may be holes in our understanding but not in the results we enjoy.
—KIP HARDING

From the Kids

A Glance at Childhood
By Serennah Harding (written at age 15)
[2006]

My family has an amazing story, and people have always been interested in how we've come to be. My mother took it upon herself to make this thought a reality. I'm just here to help.

Every day Mom would try and write something in her spiral-bound notebook, in between schooling the five-year-old and answering phone calls. Most often, she only had time to write a few sentences, maybe a couple of paragraphs, but they were always in the same used notebook with missing pages. It probably belonged to one of my siblings for journaling. In a large family, everything gets re-used. My old third-grade math notebook is now my little brother's essay-writing companion, only the first thirty pages have been torn out.

My parents have found that, like a good notebook, one's parenting and teaching skills must be re-used if they have proved themselves successful. Not every family is bound together by the same principles, disciplines, or our kind of love. In any case, it takes a lot of emotional, physical, and mental work to keep a family together as long as needed to prepare children for their future lives. This is required first by the parents and eventually by the children if they wish to lead successful lives of their own. A parent cannot plant desire in a child, but a parent can foster it.

There are many facets of a child's personality that need fostering. I can only name them through personal experience as a child, not as a parent, even though I feel I've raised a couple

in my time! A child needs emotional stability, reasonable intelligence, physical and mental health, and to be loved. My parents
never failed on that last one, and because of it, my siblings and
I aren't lacking severely in the others. Although, I'd have to say
that on a practical level, my parents were far from parenting experts when our family began and aren't experts even now (sorry,
Mom and Dad, I'm just speaking the truth).

4

No Do-Overs

Listen to advice and accept discipline, and at the end you will be
counted among the wise.
—PROVERBS 19:20

Change is inevitable, especially for a military family. We were soon reassigned to Maxwell Air Force Base in Alabama. Hannah was able to transfer to Auburn University at Montgomery (AUM) without a high school transcript or an SAT score because she had plenty of transfer credits (over twenty-six credit hours). Some universities will allow you to come in as a "transfer student" and will not require a transcript or an SAT score if you meet the credit requirements. This may have been different if we were attempting to send our daughters straight to a four-year university. In essence, transfer credits have become our main "back door" to college.

Rosannah had to transfer to Troy State University in Montgomery (TUM), which is now called Troy University, because she had fewer credit hours. After two semesters she was able to join her older sister at AUM. (Incidentally, Kip got his master of science in management [MSM] degree from Troy University two years later.) This was much better for our family because she could be on campus with her older sister. They could take classes together, and there weren't as many night classes. TUM had mostly evening classes because it was more of an adult school. But there was a definite advantage to her being with adults. Her classmates were busy working people who did not ask my daughter very many questions. This can be a good thing if one is concerned about how a thirteen-year-old can relate to adults. Most of the conversations were about class material, not so much about personal issues.

Our daughters were only on campus for classes or for short periods between class times to study in the library or the computer lab. They were not joining the sororities or going to the weekend parties. Most of their socializing was with church friends, family friends, neighbors, and their own siblings and relatives. They were actually spending more time with our family than if they had been attending a public high school. The high school experience turns into trying to fit in, a lot of "hanging out," after-school activities, and club commitments. Students' lives are consumed with high school gossip, lots of homework—and no college credit.

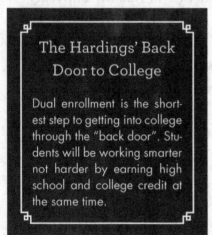

The Hardings' Back Door to College

Dual enrollment is the shortest step to getting into college through the "back door". Students will be working smarter not harder by earning high school and college credit at the same time.

We figured out that we could get through the high school subjects more efficiently and in less time. Our kids could start earning those very important college credits sooner. They still get lots of homework but they are now working toward their degrees. Once someone gains acceptance into college, it is almost as if their high school transcript is erased, because most college freshmen have to take all the same general-education classes anyway. With our method, we end up with teenagers who are not completely peer-dependent and who still value what their parents have to say. The opinions of their friends and teachers do not take precedence. They can think on their own and value their parents' opinions.

Homeschooling and attending college early is very consistent with our philosophy of wanting our children to maximize their time with the family. We want them to be critical thinkers who won't just follow a crowd.

So to answer that famous question "What about socialization?" we want *positive* socialization. We do not want the kind of socialization where a child is in a type of school environment over seven and a half hours a day (including the bus rides), being socialized by other kids their same age. This has never made sense to us. Why would any parent want their child to learn social skills this way? We prefer to train up our own children rather than just let it happen by chance. By *chance* I mean just hoping that the child gets a good teacher this year, or just hoping that they'll make good friends this year who will share the family's values instead of being the bad influences we hear so much about in movies and the news. We only get one chance at raising our kids. There are no do-overs. We want to have a positive influence on our kids while we still can.

SO TO ANSWER THAT FAMOUS QUESTION "WHAT ABOUT SOCIALIZATION?" WE WANT *POSITIVE* SOCIALIZATION.

When we moved to Montgomery, Alabama, we thought we had all of our bases covered in regard to educational opportunities with having six universities in one city (Troy, Auburn University at Montgomery, Huntingdon College, Alabama State University, Southern Christian University [now called Amridge University], and Faulkner University). But Rosannah's choice of major was architecture, and would you believe none of those universities in the city of Montgomery offered an architecture program? Depending on where you live, this may not be a problem or you may be willing to relocate.

Homeschooling our kids and starting college early has actually maximized the amount of time we spend with our kids and minimized outside influences. The exception to this was our daughter Rosannah. Her college schedule was such that it required evening classes to stay on track at Troy, which catered to working adults. Then when her education became more specialized into an architecture program, we allowed her to move into apartments and dormitories an hour away in Auburn, Alabama (hold your breath, parents—it was risky but it turned out okay).

Then our independent young lady wanted to do the Rural Studio in western Alabama, a competitive program to build an actual house as part of an Auburn University–sponsored semester. By the time she had gained this much independence, she was ready for semesters in San Francisco and lived in a dorm room in Oakland.

Rosannah completed the spring semester (2005) at Rural Studio and then Kip (still in the air force) got active duty orders to work as an acquisitions officer for the Defense Contract Management Agency (DCMA) with Lockheed Martin in Sunnyvale, California. Hannah had to take one last summer class to complete her degree at AUM, so Rosie got her driver's license on August 2 (her birthday), Hannah walked across the stage on August 6 as AUM's youngest graduate in their history at age seventeen, then we drove out of Montgomery on August 7. Rosie drove one of our three vehicles across the U.S. as soon as the ink on her driver's license dried because I was in the backseat nursing and caring for two-month-old Mariannah.

When we arrived in California, Rosannah was just barely old enough to be allowed to move into her dorm in Oakland. Yes, that is the same Oakland with one of the highest crime rates in the nation. We were living in Sunnyvale at the time and she would take the train home on the weekends. (Okay, parents, now you can gasp.) We were torn the entire time, weighing the benefits versus the costs. But Kip always left it up to God and his daughter's choice in the end. This is what she wanted, and we did not want to get in the way.

Both our daughters Rosannah and Hannah used the CHSPE to get into college early. By taking this exam, they received their high school diplomas from the state of California. Since the CHSPE is unique to California, our third daughter, Serennah, had to take the SAT instead. At the age of eleven, she scored just high enough to be admitted to Auburn University at Montgomery with a high school transcript. Her first college class, at the age of twelve, was a summer Spanish class in which both of her sisters were with her. I remember dropping her off and asking if she wanted me to wait in the parking lot for her. She said no and was very happy and excited, without overwhelming college anxiety. She and her sisters had worked out a plan to study Spanish at the library together after class. She and Rosannah would study while Hannah was in another class. Then they would switch while Rosannah went to her class. In other words, she was never left alone.

Families with more than one child can use this creative class-scheduling technique to benefit the younger ones. But it really was done more by the grace of God than our own ingenuity in planning. I would pick all three of them up in the afternoon after all the classes were done. It was a beautiful thing to see them grow closer as they would hang out together on campus and study together at home. As we added more classes to Serennah's schedule the next semester, we would combine classes whenever we could. This resulted in good old-fashioned all-nighters before midterms and finals. They really have never literally stayed up all night. But they have enjoyed one another's company past midnight. I remembered all-nighters from high school and they were a lot of fun, mostly socializing. Studying is always more fun with friends. It was such a blessing to see the girls growing closer and really relying on one another for help. The oldest, Hannah, is always the math tutor. The second-oldest, Rosannah, took physics before the other two did, so she could tutor on that subject. And Spanish really clicked with the youngest of the first three girls, Serennah. To this day, she has taken the most Spanish classes and is the most proficient in Spanish among her siblings, so she helps the others with that.

I point out our daughters' strong suits not to show favoritism but to show how they are each gifted in different ways, like all of our children. This brings up the subject of the absence of sibling rivalry.

As each of our daughters excelled with her learning and began to show an interest in different subjects, it became quite evident that there were some areas in which each was talented. As I mentioned before, Rosannah had an artistic gift and was able to draw beautifully. Hannah enjoyed taking the same art classes, but she knew that this was probably not her strongest area. However, we still did not discourage her in taking art classes. On the contrary, it fulfilled a requirement as an elective and let her explore another side of her education. But it was okay for the family to very matter-of-factly acknowledge that she probably wasn't going to be an artist, nor did she desire to be one.

Hannah's brain was wired for math. She and her father would talk at length about complex math problems. The more advanced she became in this area, the more my husband loved for her to teach and explain to him some of the advanced math she was learning. It soon became very obvious that this was her gift. Now, Kip is a very talented poet and painter. But he also likes numbers and complex number squares. I can't say that I could ever write a poem. I do like the neatness of algebra and ending up with $x =$ some nice number. But if x has to be something abstract, I would rather quit and go read an interesting biography. I love to read about health and nutrition or any kind of book that will help me be a better mom, a better wife, or a better teacher.

Kip and I used our own talents and interests to help shape each of our children's talents and abilities, and you should apply yours in the education of your children as well. We not only dared them to dream but we rewarded them for doing so. Our kids saw what we loved to do. For instance, our children see how much Kip and I love to read. We all love to dance, so we blast a variety of music (mostly hip-hop) and have an occasional dance party in the living room. So while we might not all be artists or musicians, we can still respect and encourage the tastes of others (and have fun in the process). If you love literature, use that to guide your child in writing and learning about the great authors. They will find what they love through your guidance.

Our children are like everybody in this life. Every person is good at something. We encourage this while we discourage competition.

We motivate our children to find what they are good at, and then we help them improve in this area. We inspire in the areas where there already is much inspiration, and this sparks an interest in other things.

. . . .

Genius is an exceedingly common human quality,
probably natural to most of us.
—JOHN TAYLOR GATTO

From the Kids

Troublesome Threesome
by Serennah Harding (written at age 15)
[2006]

My father married at eighteen and hadn't any parenting experience, even after growing up with two younger brothers and three older ones. He married my mother, also eighteen at the time, and she had only her mom's example to follow. I remember my dad practicing some specific "tricks of the trade," and whether they were passed down through parents or grandparents, I do not know. I think they were made up on the fly. But they stemmed from an instinct that we should just be kind and loving toward each other. Wow . . . what a concept!

When it was just my two sisters and I roaming the house for almost five years before our brothers came around, we each had a position, a duty. Hannah, the oldest, would devise some "grand" misguided scheme. Rosie, the mediator, would follow and drag me along. And I, the youngest, would not object. As you can imagine, most often, all three of us got in trouble at the same time. After our dastardly plan crumbled upon itself, my dad would give us the benefit of the doubt and we each got to speak our piece. Even if that meant simply pulling out the pacifier and crying, "Please, Daddy, no!" That was my line. Rosie would go next and all she could think of saying, like Eve in the Garden of Eden, was, "Sorry, Daddy, Hannah made me do it." What do you do with "faking-sorry" children? Then, Hannah would plead her case and lead the way to "time-out." Of course, we all went to different places, one to the bathroom, one to the kitchen, and the other to her room. Hence the term "divide and conquer." If we ever refused to go to time-out, then "spare the rod and spoil the child" would come into play. Rosie and I would look at each other with tears in our eyes and hug under Dad's request. We would apologize again, even to Hannah, and she would come out of time-out to apologize as well, this time truthfully. After our four-way group hug (and even kisses on each cheek), I would pop my pacifier back in my mouth, Dad would wipe my teary cheek, and then I'd stroll away none the worse off. Rosie would wipe her glasses clean, move her hair out of her face, and walk back to the table to finish her drawing. By then, Hannah would already be outside climbing halfway up the tree, figuring out how to swing herself over the top of the playhouse.

That's how it always went; false confessions, punishment, true apologies, hugs, kisses, then return to work or play. Even to this day, it has always worked. In a way, my dad let us solve our own problems. He'd help us along, but it was up to us to get to resolution at our own pace, so that it would be true resolution. No fake apologies accepted. If we didn't want to apologize, just like not wanting to eat our veggies, then my dad would say "just go ahead and starve," like the Beast from Disney. We couldn't and wouldn't be happy until an apology was made.

5

Keeping Track with Transcripts

These commandments that I give you today are to be on your hearts.
Impress them on your children. Talk about them when you sit at
home and when you walk along the road, when you lie down and
when you get up.
—DEUTERONOMY 6:6–7

Let's talk about transcripts for a moment. This can be a daunting thing for many homeschooling parents. Here are some things we've done for transcripts (and we're including copies of some of the kids' transcripts at the end of the book, which you may find helpful).

Before we talk about these, we'd like to share what constitutes a "course" in each subject and how a child completes them.

Basically, our kids bounced around grade levels and courses depending on their interests and abilities. So, under the "ninth grade" we have the courses that were ninth-grade level regardless of when they took them. The courses are listed as they progressed academically from the ninth to the tenth and so on. We did not think that there was anything unethical about doing it this way because our kids were not the typical age in the "ninth grade" anyway. And some kids may be in the twelfth grade in English but not in math. Also, it may not take a full "school year" to finish a course, so the date is not as important anyway. You may even need to spread out a course over a typical "school year" if extra time is needed. The point is that they completed the course.

The easiest way to complete a course in any subject is to buy a boxed curriculum. By "boxed" we mean that it literally comes to you in a box in the mail. Just as one example, we have already recommended Alpha Omega products (AOP.com) as an easy place to start. Each box has the grade level printed on the front so you know what level of work your child is doing. Once your child is finished reading all of the workbooks and taking the quizzes and tests in the back of each workbook (if you so choose), then the child is done. It is really up to the parent to decide if the student needs to have 70 percent, 80 percent, or 100 percent proficiency before moving on. We believe in going over the material until our children understand all of the material. We are not teaching the material just for the grade.

> WE BELIEVE IN GOING OVER THE MATERIAL UNTIL OUR CHILDREN UNDERSTAND ALL OF THE MATERIAL.

Over the years, we have collected many college textbooks and use those as high school curricula. When we are not able to teach the advanced material to the level of 100 percent understanding, the kids know how to go to the Internet to look things up. Once they have worked through one college textbook, we are satisfied that they have earned high school credit for that course.

Another great evaluation tool that gives our students English credit is having our kids write a paper or write a chapter summary for what they are reading. This proves that they are understanding the material. Some of our kids like answering the questions in the back of books and taking the quizzes. Others just like to write. If we are using a "real" book from the library (not a textbook), then there will not be questions and quizzes at the back of the book. A book report can be a good evaluation tool. The child can read a whole set of history books that will equal a course. Or if your kids want to read real biographies, then perhaps the biographies can be supplemented with a textbook that gives an overview of the time period being studied. We, personally, enjoy the biographies more than the textbooks.

The same applies to science. A general science book from the library is a good place to start. We do not mind if our child quickly finishes the general science book and chooses to check out books that go into greater detail in a particular area, e.g., anatomy, creation science, physics. As long as there is learning going on, we count it. Parents will have to figure out for themselves what they will require from their students and how much material will satisfy a course requirement.

The "bouncing around" that we do is because of what we have learned. We have learned that it is easier, much more fun, and more efficient to let kids pick what they want to work on and when they want to do it. Every day we try to study the Bible, do math, write, and read. The fun and freedom is in the reading. The kids choose to read books about history, science, and any subjects that they are uniquely interested in—computers, music, drama, etc. If they get immersed in a history book, they can skip reading science for a few days or weeks until they are done with that history book or set of books. We are keeping track of how much reading they are doing and filling in the transcript as we go. The order in which they do the work is not too important. We believe that it is more important that they stay motivated about learning. Giving them some choices helps to maintain a high level of motivation. They will eventually cover everything that we have agreed upon together to put on their transcript and graduate.

This is the beauty of homeschooling. You can tailor their education to fit their needs and interests. As long as, in the end, their transcript accurately shows what they learned at the high school level, then it is fine. Some homeschoolers use portfolios, which include samples of their work. However, some of their work may be more like "service learning," where they are learning by doing. Or they may be in an apprenticeship, which might resemble the type of learning that the Bible speaks of in Deuteronomy 6:6–7.

So far, AUM, Huntingdon College, and Faulkner University have all accepted our homeschool transcripts. In 2003, Troy University did not, but that was more because they could not get past our daughter's age at the time. Serennah was twelve. They said that they could not accept "unofficial transcripts." Our daughter's transcript was not coming directly from our cover school (which functions like an umbrella of a local church). It was coming directly from us. So we just took our business elsewhere and she started at AUM and then graduated from Huntingdon at the age of seventeen. Fortunately, though, we did get to speak to a Troy University recruiter recently (in 2013) who was excited to inform us that they have changed their policy and do accept a homeschool transcript from the parent. Alabama State University, however, still has not changed its policy of requiring an ACT score of 20 for homeschoolers with an "unofficial" transcript. If a student attends a *public* school, the student only needs a 15 on the ACT.

• • •

Continuing our journey into homeschooling and having our kids reaching college by twelve, it was completely natural for Serennah to want to do what her sisters had done. There was a catch, though, since we were now living in Alabama. There was no high school proficiency exam in this state, as there had been in California. I had called the surrounding states and there were no such exams there, either. There was only the GED, and you had to be between the ages of sixteen and eighteen in some of these states to take it, if I remember correctly. I am thankful that we were stationed in California when our oldest daughter was ready to pursue higher education. The CHSPE may be a hassle when you're trying to declare true independence from high school, but it was a valid certificate, once completed, that served as some piece of legitimacy we could use in our child's favor in further enrollments.

I researched the local universities in Montgomery and found that they had dual-enrollment programs, but the SAT scores required for high school students were much higher than for high school graduates. So it is interesting that public high schoolers are being discouraged from enrolling in advanced education with requirements that are harder to meet. In our opinion, this is one more way to dumb down kids by holding them back.

I had heard a speaker at a homeschool conference talk about transcripts and how to go about putting one together. I got the idea that everything that is "high school level" can go on the student's "official" transcript. I put the word "official" in quotes because I have found that it is really up to the university to decide if it is official enough. As I mentioned, Troy University would not recognize my daughter's transcript as being "official." Yet, the other two universities had no problem with it. So you can work with your cover school or any homeschool organization to make it "official." But really it comes down to figuring out what your desired university wants.

When first working on these transcripts, I searched online for basic formats. Most of what I did was formatted from my own high school transcript. As I dug my old transcript out, I realized that there can be a huge disparity among transcripts. At my high school there were those kids who were applying to Stanford and UCLA. Their transcripts included advanced placement (AP) physics, AP chemistry, calculus, and many extracurricular activities. I know because I hung out with these folks. Then there were the ones who were going to graduate with the bare-minimum requirements. They may have started with prealgebra and ended up with a consumer math class. I hung out with these folks, too, mostly at parties. Then there were others who had plenty of intelligence but didn't get inspired by what their school was offering. In other words, a transcript that a homeschool parent creates must be authentic and fit among the plethora of public education students' transcripts.

Take Kip and me, for instance. We were very different. He felt uninspired by school. I wanted to go to Santa Clara University. I was above average among the students because I was able to earn some AP credits. The point is that not everyone's transcript has to look alike and not everyone's home life is conducive to learning, either. As a homeschooling parent, one has to truthfully grade one's children based on an honest appraisal of their work.

In our case, our two oldest never needed a transcript because they went from being sophomores in home high school to being dual-enrolled at a community college that didn't require a transcript. Then they tested for their high school diploma (CHSPE), which didn't require a transcript. And finally they attended the community college full-time until they had enough credits to transfer to a four-year institution. At this juncture, the four-year institution did not require a high school transcript because they had enough college credits to be considered transfer students. This is that "back door" into college for homeschoolers if you choose to use it and if it applies in your area.

What matters most is that they can do the college-level work when they get there, not that you have to be creative in making a high school transcript. We have done it both ways (with and without a transcript) and feel we have made no breach of integrity in our children's records or education.

An important point here is that we believe in 100 percent teaching—that is, teaching until a child can earn an A in the subject matter. If I'm going to give a grade for something, my child is going to learn the material until they earn an A. This explains our 4.0 averages for Serennah and Heath. Our school philosophy is to teach educational material until we know the children have mastered the subject matter for the future. If we're confident they have got the skills to complete a certain math level or English level, we press forward to the next level. We don't want the child to get bogged down or bored. Conversely, we want each child to research and explore to the greatest degree those things that truly interest that particular child.

The girls excelled in college, but had they been in public school, I'm sure their transcripts may have suffered from the public school educational system, which holds a

> ## A Harding School Math Course
>
> Math starts with counting how many Cheerios landed outside of your child's bowl in the morning. By working consistently in workbooks every day, your child can quickly learn to carry the one, borrow, do long division, etc. In each subject the child should get an A to pass the course. Math can end with earning that minimum score on the ACT/SAT to start college.

different teaching philosophy. Public schools allow students to earn grades that are less than an A, letting them move on when they haven't mastered the skills they need. There are just too many students in the classes. Teachers cannot give the individual attention that is required to help *all* students earn A's. I believe education should be pass/fail, only no one is allowed to fail; they simply have to retake that subject. And subjects should not go for whole semesters. Courses can be completed in several weeks or a couple of months at a time, according to your child's interest and ability.

Weaving through subjects in homeschooling is a wonderful method of keeping kids interested. Educators can reel children in to be interested in any particular area in which the educator feels the child is lacking by mixing subject matters. The challenge in this is later reflecting that on a transcript, but with integrity, a parent will know how to rate a child's abilities on this important document.

As soon as we knew that Alabama would be different for Serennah, we started "filling in" her transcript. She was eleven and doing a lot of high school–level work. We went back and documented all high school–level work that she had done up to that point. Then we started to make sure that everything she did from this point on was at a high school level so that it could be put on her transcript. The next few kids started working on their high school transcripts between the ages of eight and nine in the subjects where they were ready. This is one of the keys to getting to college by twelve: work on that high school transcript as soon and as quickly as possible. It should not have to take four whole

> THIS IS ONE OF THE KEYS TO GETTING TO COLLEGE BY TWELVE: WORK ON THAT HIGH SCHOOL TRANSCRIPT AS SOON AND AS QUICKLY AS POSSIBLE.

years to cover four years of high school, especially if you homeschool all year-round.

Serennah was a great student. I could give her a stack of books and tell her what I was going to require. I would tell her to read each book, write me a paper on it, answer the questions at the ends of the chapters, or take the tests or quizzes at the ends of the chapters. Whatever it was that I required, she would crank it out. She was also studying for the SAT and took it in December of 2002 at the age of eleven. She knew what she had to do to meet the enrollment requirements at AUM, so she was self-motivated to do what her sisters had done.

This is where I have to say that it was so important that she could see herself in college by twelve. Kip and I knew she could do it, but she had to believe it and want it. It would have been too hard to "push" her through high school. I do not think that one can push a child and get the same great results. They must be inspired! She wanted to be a doctor and knew it was going to be a long, hard road. We totally supported her and helped her in pursuing her dream. This was *her* dream, not ours.

From the Kids

A Day in the Life
by Serennah Harding (written at age 15)
[2006]

From our living room sofa, you see something different. There I sit. Katrinnah carries a rather large newly purchased package of paper towels to the kitchen. Its height matches hers, and it shields her eyes from sight. Her toe is bumped on the book chest as she makes her way down the hallway. Meanwhile, Heath sits at the computer—typing away. Keith is now coming in and out of the kitchen. He claims he is thirsty, but more likely it is the fact that the book he was reading is now dull. Mom is sitting with Mariannah. She is checking her for a dirty diaper while filing through paperwork—a skill all mothers master by child number five. Katie runs in to tell Mommy that she ate her fruit after lunch while she was out. They both are very proud.

These sights do not surprise me. Although unusual, they are exactly what I would expect to occur here—anything and everything. No day in the Harding home ever repeats itself quite the same. The living room is our schoolroom, guest entertaining quarters, movie theater, dance studio, debate center, and newsroom. We started posting family memos on the refrigerator for a time, but shortly after we found a more efficient method of making things known.

Occasionally, you'll see the three-year-old skipping/running throughout the house with her handmade megaphone shouting, "Come and get some food before it's taken!" If you learn anything in this house it's how to finish all your food before leaving the table because you'll rarely find it still there upon return. No one is ever starving here, so the thief probably just needed your mashed potatoes to putty his toothpick castle—a valid reason. Your food, however, is not the only thing that should be under your watchful eye.

If you're one who needs a stool to brush your teeth each night, be careful. A few hours earlier, an ingenious mastermind may have reconstructed the leaning tower of Pisa in the kitchen with your stool as the foundation. The cookies on top of the fridge needed rescuing.

6

All for One and One for All

My child, if you are wise then I will be happy. I will be pleased if
you speak what is right.
—PROVERBS 23:15–16

The chair in the college classroom felt familiar. For a moment, I (Mona Lisa) closed my eyes and remembered sitting in the back of Kip's intermediate algebra class twenty years earlier while I was pregnant with our first child. Could two decades really have passed so quickly? I couldn't stop fidgeting and I knew it was nerves. Heath was starting Intermediate Algebra/Math 105 at Foothill College in California.

Heath was ten years old.

I wondered what Heath's instructor would be like. How would he react to a ten-year-old sitting in his room? Would he give him a hard time, or would he choose to ignore him altogether? What if he made a joke at Heath's expense in front of the rest of the class? What if he bullied and badgered Heath? I knew our firstborn son was strong like his father, but still . . . he was only ten years old. Would the instructor eventually say, "I'm sorry, but you can't leave a ten-year-old in my class unsupervised"?

It didn't matter if he did. I was prepared to stay in the class by having my oldest daughter stay in the van with the sleeping sixteen-month-old.

I closed my eyes again and asked God for peace.

The second evening of Heath's class, I waited outside in the chilly car in the parking lot. I had six kids at home, but I was there at this college for this fourth child. This routine would prove to be typical. And this philosophy proved to be the norm: we do all that we can to help the one child who needs us the most at the time. Heath was ten years old, so I spent every Monday and Wednesday of that semester waiting on him—occasionally wracked with worry, but most of the time content to be there and enjoy the stillness. Sometimes Kip would join me and we would turn this into a date night spent at the corner coffee shop while Heath sat in class. We gave him a cell phone in case he needed anything. Throughout the process of having our kids going to college at an early age, we felt that they should always feel safe and secure. This feeling of safety and security gave them the confidence they needed to do amazing things . . . and succeed!

> WE DO ALL THAT WE CAN TO HELP THE ONE CHILD WHO NEEDS US THE MOST AT THE TIME.

When my husband took this same intermediate algebra class at Fort Riley, Kansas, almost twenty years prior, through Central Texas College, he got a C. He was in the army then, working long days and staying up late at night with our first baby. It's a lot harder to get a degree when you have a family to care for. Our kids watched their father going to school on weekends to complete his master's degree. We also explained to them how much homework we had in high school. They knew that they would be extremely busy if they were in a public or private high school. They would be there six to seven hours a day, plus there would be so many extracurricular activities in order to try to have a well-rounded transcript to get into a good college. Then there would be all of the social obligations. This was where I wasted most of my time. Too many parties. Too many boys. Too many distractions.

Heath, however, would not be distracted. He was extremely confident. We would have to keep reminding him that pride comes before a fall. This was to help him remain humble. We also told him often, "Don't be a show-off."

One of our favorite proverbs says that people will think even a fool is wise if he is quiet, but if he speaks he may prove otherwise (see Proverbs 17:28). So we advised Heath to speak only if called upon in class, and then he should speak up. But if he had a valid question, and he thought it might also benefit the class to hear the answer, then he should ask.

The first few days of Heath's classes were nerve-wracking. Normally I would have Kip make the initial contacts with people in admissions, financial aid, and the professors because they were always the most awkward. My husband is not daunted at all by anyone's title. He really believes that everyone puts on his pants one leg at a time. I, on the other hand, have my insecurities. Maybe it is because I don't have any fancy letters after my name. But since my husband and I are one, I know that God made a good match. Kip is confident enough for both of us. He is always telling me how smart I am and how I could walk into his workplace and fit right in.

Kip has always told me that I, just like anybody else, have the capacity to learn and to work with others. That, he says, is 99 percent of what a person needs to succeed in the workplace, even if that person has been a stay-at-home mom for the last twenty years. This confidence spills over to our kids. It is no cliché in our home to say, "You can be anything you want to be" or "The sky is the limit." Or "If you can dream it, you can achieve it." These quotes are so overused that other kids may not think that they apply to them. Yet they are central to the way we are raising our kids.

We do all that we can to help fund their dreams, encourage their development, and be there for them along the way to keep them on the paths of their own choosing. We have been criticized for asking our children at too young an age what they want to be when they grow up. For us, this question is a real question, not some hypothetical game for fun. We are very, very serious in asking the question. In the course of a lifetime, people change their jobs and careers several times. I expect my children might also do the same. Why not start the process early? They need to be able to rebound and follow after something worthwhile to have satisfaction and a standard of living that God would want for them in the paths they have chosen.

When Heath started college at the age of ten, not twelve like his sisters, the natural question had to be asked: "Are they getting younger?" Was the next one going to start at nine? We didn't think so, because Keith was a lot more shy than his siblings, but we still had to wonder. Yes, even though he did start algebra at age eight, who were we to say what would happen? We were not trying to break our own record. We treated each child as an individual and still do.

Having ten children does not mean we treat them like a mob. We take extra care to be sensitive to their individual needs because we know that some people think that no one can give that many children enough individual time and attention. But when my husband or I say kind words to the kids, it is like fuel for a car; it fills their tanks and they can run on it for quite some time. There is a false assumption in society that if you have many kids, they won't get enough attention. Not only is this false, but it is especially false if one homeschools. My kids get a lot of individual attention. After all, today I only have four students, not twenty to thirty, in my classroom.

> AFTER ALL, TODAY I ONLY HAVE FOUR STUDENTS, NOT TWENTY TO THIRTY, IN MY CLASSROOM.

Some might expect me to write about something people term a "child-centered home" (CCH) in order to get the results that we are getting. The idea behind a CCH is that everything revolves around the kids' lives. The parents are totally sacrificed and subordinate to the kids: driving them here and there while buying them all that they ask for. While I wholeheartedly support spending time with your kids, I am not suggesting that this should be the core of your home. You should have a "marriage-centered home" (MCH) instead! The MCH is surrounded in layers where kids and work and other important targets for our lives are prioritized. Everything fails if the marriage is not first.

There is a saying: "If Mama isn't happy, then nobody is happy." This is only half true. If Mommy *and* Daddy's relationship is not a happy one, then nobody is happy. Kids grow up feeling secure and grow up better adjusted if they see their parents are in love. Marriage takes a huge commitment and a lot of work. We really make our relationship a priority. The time that we invest in each other is time well spent. If more people would spend more time working on their marriage, their kids would reap the benefits.

At the end of Heath's first semester, he had earned an A in that course and even gotten a 100 percent on his final exam. We were all so pleased with that instructor, who made Heath feel at ease. So naturally, Heath picked him for his very next course in statistics.

See, our children aren't *just* book smart.

From the Kids

Heath (written at age 10)
[2005]

I would like to share my thoughts on the Harding home. But first I want to tell a little about myself. I enjoy reading books and going on the computer. It's tough being ten when you're living with nine other people in a small home in the Silicon Valley. The amazing part is I survive. Some of the challenges I must face in this family are phrased like this: When your mother goes to the store and comes back with a lot of food, you better eat it quick because there will only be two days of feast before famine. You also have to wait ten minutes for the "TP refill man" (a.k.a. my brother Keith) at least once every day while in the bathroom.

When you're ten, you're too old to use the excuse, "I'm younger than you and far cuter" to get what you want. And when you want to go somewhere alone, you're too young to use the explanation, "I'm older and more responsible than you. So I get to go." My older siblings like to play the card, "If you come, then all your little siblings will want to come, too." In my opinion, the only reason they tag along wherever I go is because they think I'm not one of the "older kids." And Mom likes to joke around and say, "The little ones want to follow you because you're plain popular." I'm still not buying it, but it sure is nice having so many fans.

Now I would like to share my perspective of my siblings in reverse order of age: Mariannah (age 2) is a little pigtailed blob of love, laughter, curiosity, chubbiness, and joy. She is also known as "Max," and my mom calls her Mama. The few words she can say include "awa" which means agua in Spanish, and "mama" which she and my mom say over and over when they're about to lie down together for a nap. A lot of Hispanic women call their baby girls "Mama." For what reason, this gringo is not sure?!

Katrinnah (age 4) is an almost exact replica of Hannah at that age. She is almost always happy. Although, she can have mood swings and can switch between being sad and happy very quickly. This may be acting for the most part, looking at it on the negative side, but it is also something we see in many four-year-olds.

Seth (age 6) is a boy who is stuck between growing up to be a fireman, astronaut, robot builder, construction worker, karate/sumo wrestler, and policeman. He just recently found out he needs to know how to read without any help to take on just about any occupation. As you probably know from his wanting to be a sumo wrestler, he loves to wrestle and tickle my dad.

Keith (age 8) is closer to my age than to all of the other siblings. He is also the oldest of the younger four. He just started algebra and helps Seth with his reading.

My sisters started college when they were 12. I think I am going to break their record. My goal is to start by 11. I am studying to take the CHSPE right now. I am taking acting classes right now and I want to study filmmaking in college.

7

Bring on the Naysayers

He replied, "Because you have so little faith. Truly I tell you, if you
have faith as small as a mustard seed, you can say to this mountain,
'Move from here to there,' and it will move. Nothing will be
impossible for you."
—MATTHEW 17:20

We've had critics at all stages of our homeschooling journey. This includes opposition from those trusted to
teach our children, like the time Heath faced some
prejudice from his first English professor at Foothill College in the
Bay Area.

I (Kip) remember the first time we encountered that English
professor. On the first day of class, the professor said in front of everyone, "This class requires life experience. He may not have much
to write about." It was age discrimination at its finest. He didn't care
for my dropping him off at class or for anything that this air force
captain had to say.

It brought to mind another child who was a similar age. This particular child received her diary on her thirteenth birthday. Fortunately for the world, Anne Frank found plenty to write about, and a child's voice was shown to be worthy of respect.

Heath remained strong and confident on that first day of class. I was so proud that he stood up for his rights that day and went ahead and sat in the classroom in the chair I offered to him. He was and still is my hero, just like all my children!

Fortunately, this instructor eventually came around and became friendly to our son. We knew that he would wise up when Heath proved his ability after a few writing assignments. Unfortunately, though, Heath had to learn firsthand what it is like to be treated with prejudice.

In our home, we talk of "naysayers." They are the folks who are so ready to give all the reasons why *they* could never homeschool their children or have them take college classes early. Here are some of those reasons:

1. "Your kids must be geniuses."

Kip and I (Mona Lisa) are of average intelligence and so are our kids. Our children have had very average scores on the SAT and ACT. They have high GPAs, but this is a sign of good study habits and lots of hard work. Our oldest had to go to the tutoring center all through her undergrad years. Our third daughter always studies and gets help from fellow classmates. People think that it must be genetics. But what are the chances that six of our college kids have genius genes? I don't have a PhD in education, or a degree in anything else, for that matter. I just have one year of nursing school and a few college credits.

2. "How can a twelve-year-old relate to adults?"

Homeschoolers all know that their kids relate better to kids of all ages because they are not segregated by age. Well, this proved to be true when our kids started college. They did very well relating to college-age students and professors. In the case of our daughters, their classmates were usually surprised to find out how young they were. They assumed they were juniors and seniors in high school. Our boys have had to overcome the prejudice against youths on college campuses because they physically matured slower than our girls did.

As far as relating with adults, remember that there are lots of adults who are busy working people. They're not going to ask our kids very many questions. Most of the conversations will be about class material and not personal issues.

3. "I would be afraid to have my child on a college campus."

There are ways to alleviate this worry. A parent can enroll in or audit the class, just sit in the class, sit outside the class, or sit in the lounge down the hall like we did with our son Heath. We often try to enroll an older sibling in the same class or walk around the college track during a class. If there is a will, there is a way—and giving the child a cell phone can help Mom and Dad feel better, too.

4. "My child couldn't do college-level work at twelve."

It is true that if a parent doesn't believe a child can do it, it will be nearly impossible for the child to do it on their own. But if you really see your child flying through the schoolwork and think that they can do it, challenge the child. Allow the youth to start high school–level subjects as soon as they are ready. Only you know your child best. We are writing this for those of you who need to hear, "*Yes*, your child can do it!"

5. "I don't want my kids to grow up too fast."

Our children were not joining fraternities and sororities or going to the weekend parties. Instead, they were actually spending more time with our family than if they had been attending a public high school. Our kids actually get to experience more of their childhood because they have more freedom in their education and lives. Our kids may be far ahead academically and behave maturely in a college setting, but they are still very happy and well-adjusted kids/young adults. They can still play dress-up with younger siblings as well as go out for dinner with college classmates. The trouble we find with too many publicly educated adults is their schooling robbed them permanently of a "child" within themselves. They believe all childlike behavior is wrong. It is okay to have fun, feel young, and be spontaneous at times. A homeschooled youth should never change in this manner. It only requires a more general purpose in the way in which one lives one's life. It is much less likely the homeschooled youngster will miss out on a fulfilling childhood. The reason is that traditionally schooled kids end up losing their youth in thinking they can no longer be childlike at times beyond a given age. This is very much a "stuffed shirt" adult phenomenon, one that our kids have never felt pressured by.

We think it finally comes down to this: The question is not "Can my child go to college at a younger age?" When you sit down and think about homeschooling, your questions should be as follows:

1. "Do we, as parents, believe our children can do it and can we support them?"

If you feel that this is for you, then you just have to rethink your work schedule to include homeschooling. The same holds for single moms and dads, even if you only just start with supplemental home-schooling, as one of our friends did (his child is now two grades ahead of his peers). Skipping grades can be great fun! But it does have challenges in the public school setting. Public schools can't get beyond the socialization issue, ironically enough given what they say about homeschoolers sometimes. So they will hold your child back because the bigger kids may try to take advantage of your child. But two grades is better than none. It is rare that a public school will let any child skip more than two grades. Go figure. The teachers basically cower before the child bullies.

2. "Can we make the financial sacrifices necessary?"

They really do come cheaper by the dozen when it comes to home-schooling. Most of us have seen the numbers of how much it costs to raise a child these days. And like we mentioned earlier, it costs about $500 per child to homeschool them—and the government pays almost $10,000 per child, on top of which you have to pay for all those new supplies every year. We share everything, including pencils, books, and clothes. What if you chose to spend less on certain things? What if you chose to not buy designer clothing? What if people hear you have a lot of kids and regularly give you hand-me-downs? Would you be too proud to accept them? You could hand these hand-me-downs all the way down to your last child. We have been very blessed. Our children have lots of everything. Friends and family have been very generous to us.

We try to be generous with each other, and it comes back to us tenfold. What the statistics don't show are the blessings that children bring: how they bond with one another as they learn how to do household chores, how a ten-year-old can help make lunch for a younger sibling, how a teenager can help a younger sibling with her math, and how they all know it is their job to change that diaper if they discover it needs changing.

While most teenagers are making minimum wage while working through college, homeschooled students can have their degrees and quadruple their wages. Although they may be eighteen or younger when they receive their baccalaureate degrees, they will still face the same challenges the twenty-two- or twenty-three-year-old graduates face with having little job experience. It is better to face that earlier than later. Hannah's first boss at a start-up company in Silicon Valley in California was very impressed with her intelligence and maturity even though she had no job experience. Rosannah got an even higher-paying internship job before she finished college. I say this not as an unhealthy comparison but simply to show that success follows the younger students who strike out early for themselves.

We love having all of the teenagers around because it is very convenient to have multiple babysitters. Our adult friends are usually surprised that we get out as much as we do. They always ask, "Who's watching the kids?" Then they realize: "Oh yeah, you've got those teenage babysitters at home." The bonus is that our toddlers do not experience too much separation anxiety. Even though our girls have lots of homework to do, they are learning to separate the little ones and keep them productively busy or well entertained. This is good training for parenthood because they will have an idea of some of the sacrifices that must be made. They of course get plenty of free time, too. We (just the parents) will go see a movie as a date one night, and then the following night if the movie is good, the teenagers will have their turn to see the same one.

I'm always surprised to hear it when someone has a child who is driving age or older and the parents still don't want them to drive. I'm sure that parents like this have their reasons, but we consider a driving teenager to be a *huge* blessing. We need extra drivers in our family. It is a privilege to get to drive and we expect them to help out with all of our family activities. The laws are changing now to discriminate more against teenage drivers because of the few who behave irresponsibly. We train our young drivers well and expect them to be responsible in this very important area of life.

3. "Are we willing to do what it takes to help our child do it?"

As we stated in the beginning, we did not just want to write a how-to book. We wanted to share our story, too. If it inspires you to find out what you need to do to reach your goals (that is, if early college even becomes one of your goals), then great! We want to inspire people and would count your rekindled motivation as a success.

OUR DESIRE, IN SHARING OUR STORY, IS TO TAKE THE FEAR OUT OF FAILURE.

Yes, there are typical concerns. People thinking your children must be geniuses. Questions about how twelve-year-olds can relate to adults. Fears of leaving them on a college campus. Belief that they can never do college work. Or the worry that your kids are growing up too fast. Our desire, in sharing our story, is to take the fear out of failure.

We have been criticized by people who do not agree with what we are doing. We have been called lots of things, including "national nut jobs" by a popular blogger. Interestingly, most of the folks who commented on this particular blog were actually defending our right to educate our kids the way that we do. This particular blogger had one thing in common with all the other naysayers out there. These well-meaning folks *assume* that they know what we are about. They *assume* that Kip is some kind of a drill sergeant who wakes up our kids at the crack of dawn and makes them complete a vigorous curriculum in between doing push-ups. Though he does know how to do these things—being a former Officer Training School (OTS) instructor—this is not how he fathers.

We laugh at this with our kids and they feel that if these folks ever got a chance to actually meet and hang out with our family, a lot of misconceptions would be cleared up. We do not write all this to brag, but we think that it is pretty significant that our kids have served in leadership roles during their time in college despite the fact that they have been so much younger than their counterparts when elected.

....

Knowledge which is acquired under compulsion has no hold on the mind. Therefore do not use compulsion, but let early education be a sort of amusement; you will then be better able to discover the child's natural bent.

—PLATO

From the Kids

Heath (Age Ten) Interviews His Brothers (Five and Eight) in 2007

One day Heath (ten years old at the time), decided he'd like to add more literary diversity to our family and interviewed Seth and Keith to see what they had to say about homeschooling versus public schooling. Here are their responses to some practical questions:

Heath interviews Seth (age 5)

What things do you like about homeschooling?
•I can finish early if I'm fast. Then I get to play!
•I get a break in between some subjects.

What things do you not like about homeschooling?
•I can't get my treat until I'm done with dictation.

What things would you like if you went to a school?
•I think they have good food.
•I would like being with kids my age.

What things would you not like if you went to school?
•I would miss my parents.

Heath interviews Keith (age 8)

What things do you like about homeschooling?
• I can do my school in my bed.
•I can finish early if I'm quick.

What things do you not like about homeschooling?
•I can get easily distracted by my siblings.

What things would you like if you went to a school?
•I can be with kids my age.
•I can go on field trips more often.

What things would you not like if you went to school?
•I couldn't learn at my own pace.
•I would have to wake up early.
•I might be late.
•I wouldn't get to see my family.

8

Three Little Ladies

With this in mind, we constantly pray for you, that our God may make you worthy of His calling, and that by His power He may bring to fruition your every desire for goodness and your every deed prompted by faith. We pray this so that the name of our Lord Jesus may be glorified in you, and you in Him, according to the grace of our God and the Lord Jesus Christ.

—2 THESSALONIANS 1:11–12

In April of 2007, after twenty years of military service, Kip decided to take a separation bonus and leave the air force. He hadn't been selected for the rank of major. Since the military has a policy of "up or out," Kip retired as a reserve captain. He tends to think outside the box and individual creativity is not always rewarded in the military.

At first he circulated his résumé in Silicon Valley, but we quickly realized that it would be very difficult to have the standard of living that we had gotten used to in Alabama. We decided to go back to our seven-bedroom home in Montgomery. Kip has always said if you have to work hard in life, you might as well live where the weather is warm and you have a little elbow room. We had left Kansas because of the cold weather back in 1997 and had left California because of the small, expensive homes. He loves the beauty of the snow and wants to head to the mountains if www.slopdope.com picks up in web-traffic. We are willing to go wherever God leads first and foremost. The only thing that made us hesitate at this time was that we would be leaving three of our girls behind.

Our eldest daughter, Hannah, was nineteen and finishing up her last year of a master's degree in math at California State University, East Bay, located in Hayward. Rosannah, who was almost eighteen years old, had one year left in her five-year architecture program. Then there was Serennah, who was sixteen and thought she knew better than her parents since she decided to stay at Santa Clara University and finish her degree.

For each daughter we left behind, there were blessings and benefits that came to them. Hannah and Serennah stayed with church friends in San Jose while Rosannah stayed with Kip's wonderful aunt Mimi in San Francisco. While each of them had very good reasons for staying, this was still something we never planned on doing when we envisioned sending our kids to college by the age of twelve. This was the type of thing that kept us awake at night in prayer, praying for protection for our girls and for God's wisdom. At times I asked God for forgiveness if I thought Kip and I were doing the wrong thing.

The biggest burden probably fell on Hannah, who was studying hard to finish her degree so she could return to Alabama and help the family by hitting the workforce. With Kip no longer making that nice air force salary, Hannah's assistance would be critical. She had Serennah to motivate her every morning. Their routine would consist of Hannah dropping Serennah off at Santa Clara University, then making the hour-long commute in Bay Area traffic heading north up to Hayward. Hannah admitted being a little depressed without having all of her siblings with her. Thoughts of reuniting with her family and finally being done with school motivated her. Kip would encourage her by phone and through e-mails, reminding her of how great it was that she was getting graduate school done while she was still young. He would also remind her that when he was getting his master's degree he had the responsibility of seven children and one on the way.

Hannah and Serennah grew closer during their three months studying together and having cram sessions together. They would take "dance breaks," bake cookies, and eat snacks. On the weekends, they would have Rosannah come down from San Francisco to stay with them and would encourage her to finish her degree, too. All three of our girls were in the same "college boat," trying to realize their dreams. Sisterhood is a beautiful thing when there is no rivalry but only love and support. Hannah did eventually get to walk across the stage in June of 2007 and was treated along with her sisters to a trip to Spain by their great-aunt Mimi.

Mimi had always been a second mom to Kip growing up. She was the one who made Christmas and birthdays special for Kip and his five brothers when Kip's mom was absent due to divorce and mental illness. She owned a wonderful store on Union Street in San Francisco.

While staying with Mimi, Rosannah did very well on her own by continuing to go to church and graduating with high distinction. She fell in love with a fellow architect and we encouraged her to get married as soon as possible. Rosannah and her husband, Sergio, lived and worked in San Francisco, where he finished his master's degree.

• • •

After the graduation trip to Spain, Hannah drove with Serennah across six states to reunite with us in Alabama. She found a job doing research at Auburn University at Montgomery and took her comprehensive exam for her master's in mathematics. Unfortunately, she did not pass all sections the first time. If Hannah had been a "super genius," this could have been devastating to her. Instead, she realized that she was going to have to deal with the disappointment and study harder. She retook the exam in December and passed. At this point, the university mailed her the actual degree.

We think all kids have a much greater appreciation of their successes when they go through struggles. We are not afraid to share life's ugly details with them when things are going bad. We choose to include all of them and pray together as a family so that when God answers our prayers there is no doubt in their minds where the help is coming from. We have learned not to take things for granted when things are going well, either, and to give thanks for all that we enjoy as a family. Hannah eventually began teaching math as an adjunct professor at Auburn University at Montgomery and at Faulkner University. She was featured on a local TV station as AUM's "youngest professor," where she had this powerful quote to share:

"The biggest lie we tell ourselves is 'I can't do it,'" Hannah said to the reporter. "Now, as a teacher, I see it on the other end and I'm the one who gets to be encouraging."

When Hannah was a junior in college she read Rick Husband's biography. He was the pilot on the Columbia shuttle. She hoped that pursuing a PhD in engineering would help her get into the program as a mission specialist. So during this time, she continued to search for a way into NASA. God brought along another wonderful

"THE BIGGEST LIE WE TELL OURSELVES IS 'I CAN'T DO IT.'"

opportunity for her to pursue graduate work while having her tuition paid. In addition, she received a stipend while at Tuskegee University. She did research for the university for two years and learned a lot. Unfortunately, her adviser was an extremely strict man. He pushed Hannah very hard, but not always in a positive direction. She became a much stronger person while working under this scrutiny. However, the situation caused her to look long and hard at what her goals were. After much prayer, she came to the realization that her dream was still to work for NASA and not necessarily to get a PhD at this time under difficult educational circumstances.

God really blessed Hannah once again by allowing her to gracefully leave the university with a master's degree in mechanical engineering in May of 2010. With a second master's, she had a much more competitive résumé.

Once she filled out the paperwork to leave school, Kip was laid off from his job. We now had two unemployed people in the family. Hannah could not even collect unemployment because she was not having any taxes taken out of her stipend as a research graduate student. Now she owed the IRS. Everywhere we looked people were being laid off, businesses were closing, and all NASA programs were about to undergo massive spending cuts, shutting down the space shuttle program entirely. Hannah had to talk to God about giving her a new vision. This was a very tough time for her.

After a few months of unemployment, Hannah accepted a position as a high school math teacher at a private Christian school for less than thirty hours per week. This was a great financial hardship as well as a personal challenge. She was used to teaching adults at the college level who were in the classroom willingly and ready to learn. She was shocked to learn of all the drama associated with teenagers, even at a Christian school. As a homeschooler, she had personally skipped this whole peer-dependent teen scene. She operated on the love of family. Immaturity and disrespect were never tolerated in our home as she was growing up. So she was really disappointed that not all teenagers are excited about having the privilege of an education. What she knew about the "craziness" of high school she got from movies, but even then we chose to watch more intelligent films. She learned quickly that her influence as a teacher would be limited.

Those days were challenging for twenty-three-year-old Hannah because she was a good teacher who genuinely cared about the whole student. She was sensitive enough to get wrapped up in the lives of her students. There were many evenings where she would come home and share her day with tears in her eyes. All that we could do as parents was to listen and encourage her to do only what she could. We reminded her that she could not solve all of the world's problems in a day. She could be a positive influence in the classroom, but she had no control over what went on outside of the classroom. Thankfully, she did have the freedom to share her faith in God with these kids (most of whom were not Christians) because she was at a Christian school.

Hannah decided to move on at the end of the school year because she could barely pay her bills on a part-time teacher's salary. She was hoping to find employment in Birmingham and to share a place with her sister Serennah. Instead, she accepted a position in San Jose, California, as a quality assurance technician. It was difficult to not have our "right-hand girl" around with us anymore after she left. (In the latest turn of events, she is back at Tuskegee working on a doctorate degree. She lives just down the street from us in our rental home and is reinvigorated to take her scientific knowledge to the next level.)

Rosannah's journey was quite different, because she never wanted to move with us to California in the first place.

After earning all of the general-education credits that she could while we lived in Montgomery, Alabama, Rosannah applied to Auburn University. Just days before her fifteenth birthday she found out she was accepted. Her quinceañera (which is a young Latina's celebration of her fifteenth birthday) was bittersweet as we celebrated her "coming out" and her moving out. We absolutely love these parties and are really looking forward to the family celebrations for Katrinnah, Mariannah, and Lorennah, who will turn fifteen in 2018, 2020, and 2022 respectively. It's like a big family reunion, a backyard barbecue (depending on the time of year), and an all-out get-back-to-your-cultural-roots kind of thing. The food is incredible. Latin cervezas, a DJ or mariachis playing, piñatas, streamers, balloons, and a huge cake are all part of the fun. Too bad the boys don't have some kind of equivalent in our heritage, but we're only English, Spanish, and Welsh to my knowledge. We know celebrating cultural heritage is a wonderful way to bring family together and to educate everyone on history and have a really fun time in the process. We enjoy family gatherings so much that we even celebrate half birthdays, although with somewhat less preparation!

Going back to Rosannah, we networked and found a female graduate student who would allow Hannah and Rosannah to rent a room from her. The apartment was a bike ride away from campus, which was an hour from our home in Montgomery. Hannah transferred to this main campus to accompany Rosannah and to drive both of them home every weekend. The plan was for me to drive out to stay with them every Wednesday evening with the nursing baby, Katrinnah. This would be an ideal way to check on them in the middle of the week. I ended up going a couple of times during the week because Rosannah needed the extra emotional support.

The summer course Rosannah was taking was a sort of architectural boot camp. The university accepted way more students than they intended to accept in the fall so they could put them through vigorous course work and watch which students caved under the pressure and quit. Kip and I had both been through boot camp ourselves, so we were able to explain their tactics. The assignments were almost impossible (e.g., she had to build a sphere out of string and glue!). We spent many evenings in hobby stores trying to find materials and meet requirements. All I could do was encourage her to do her best and turn *something* in. I also helped to keep her awake into the wee hours of the morning while her models dried.

Some of Rosannah's models turned out pretty good, while others literally flopped over. She quickly learned that *not quitting* was half the battle. The class got smaller and smaller almost daily. It turned out that those who did not quit and did their best were admitted in the fall to the program. At the age of fifteen, she was one of the forty students who made it. There were one hundred and twenty who started the 2004 summer "weed-out" program.

> SHE QUICKLY LEARNED THAT *NOT QUITTING* WAS HALF THE BATTLE.

After a semester at the main campus, Rosannah was accepted into the Rural Studio program, where she would actually take part in building a home for a needy family in a rural setting. This type of hands-on experience was an amazing way to learn.

Once again, Rosannah was pushing us out of our comfort zone by wanting to try new and challenging things. We didn't fault her for this because this is part of who she is. Our kids are not afraid to try new things. Rosa was only our second child in college at the time so we had a lot of things to figure out for ourselves. We were able to have a heart-to-heart with the house mother where the female students would be staying. We felt very comfortable that Rosannah would be properly supervised while studying an hour and a half from home.

In 2005, when the semester was over, we had to insist that she come with us to California for Kip's next military assignment. I (Mona Lisa) had to basically force her to hand over the materials I needed to get her application and portfolio in to California College of the Arts (CCA). The college had just changed its name from College of Arts and Crafts. When Rosannah heard that she cried some more and resisted the move because she did not think it was a "real" architecture school. We had to enlist Kip's aunt Mimi to visit the school personally and find out from her own circles if the school was legitimate.

Once she got the list of professional architects who were also the teaching staff at CCA from Aunt Mimi, Rosa started to get excited. This is an amazing part of the program at CCA. The staff are working professionals. Some of them even own their own firms and work in the field while teaching. This was an asset, because she was able to find work easily as an intern during her last year and then professionally after graduation.

We now laugh about how we dragged Rosie to California "kicking and screaming" and then, funny enough, she ended up not wanting to ever leave. Parents everywhere can probably relate to having teenagers second-guess them. Sometimes they have to hear the truth somewhere else. You gotta love 'em.

Now that Rosannah has been married for four years and working for five, she has decided to temporarily leave her beloved San Francisco and attend a one-year master's program at Cooper Union in New York City. She called me one day to ask me if I thought she should apply to their very competitive full-ride program. Of course I had to encourage her to follow her dreams. This is always the answer.

• • •

Like Rosannah, Serennah didn't want to leave college to move with us. After many tearful discussions, we convinced her to come home with us. She was in her junior year at age sixteen. This was April of 2007, when Kip was retiring and leaving the air force. Serennah was attending Santa Clara University (SCU) and living at home with us in Sunnyvale, California. She wanted to stay one more year to graduate from SCU. We left California that April but the girls stayed to finish the spring semester.

We went through a lot of heartache with Rosannah leaving the home so young. Even though it turned out okay in the end, we were not ready to part with Serennah. College can have a way of magnetizing your children toward their goals and it makes it hard if you have to change their routine. Rosannah had left Alabama very upset when the air force moved us to California in 2005. Later she thanked us for "forcing" her to come with us to California. Now Serennah thanks us for "forcing" her to come back to Alabama.

We found out about the doctor of osteopathy (DO) program from a friend out here in Alabama and it has been a great blessing to Serennah. This move cost Serennah an extra semester at Huntingdon College but we knew it was important that we should all stay together as much as possible. Because Rosannah was turning eighteen in August of 2007 and only had one semester left to complete her degree, we thought she should stay and rely on Aunt Mimi to be the loving extended family member that she was to Kip as a child.

After their great-aunt Mimi took the three girls to Spain, Serennah had to come home and take an online crash review course before taking the Medical College Admission Test (MCAT) right after her trip. She did not do so great and it caused a delay in her going straight to medical school. She then spent many hours applying to several traditional medical schools without acceptance. There were lots of application fees to pay and essays to write. She also began to work in our physician's ob-gyn clinic as a Spanish translator. Her Spanish really began to improve.

After several rejection letters from medical schools, God let our path cross (literally, as we walked a path at the park) with that of a friend who happened to work for an association that recruits students into the field of osteopathic medicine. What a blessing. We had never even heard of osteopathic medicine. Serennah was so skeptical. She didn't even want to entertain the idea of not going to a "traditional" medical school. Once again, Dad had to have that "just trust me" talk with her. She trusted her dad once again and talked to the recruiter friend. She agreed to apply once she found out that a doctor of osteopathy (DO) has to undergo the same basic training and board exams that an MD has to take. It is basically a different approach to medicine, more whole-body and hands-on rather than relying heavily on medications. In our research we also discovered that the military will accept a DO and an MD interchangeably. This was right in line with our own ideas of medicine anyway, so we had a providentially perfect fit. And it was another kind of back door we had discovered!

Serennah has become very wise beyond her years. I believe that part of this is due to the fact that she knows how to pray over a matter, give it to God, and then trust in God's plan. Very often she will call to ask for Kip's advice in matters concerning life in general, but many times she wants to know how her dad would deal with "people issues." In her senior year of college she was chosen to be a Huntingdon College ambassador, or class representative. She would fill many leadership roles even later in medical school. She is very articulate and outgoing. I know that she gets her ability to speak in front of crowds from her father. She is usually very intuitive about how to deal with people much older than her. We think it is because, as our third child, she followed her sisters around, observing how they handled matters, yet she had many opportunities to lead her younger siblings, too.

In May of 2008, she became one of Huntingdon College's youngest graduates at the age of seventeen. The university could not confirm who their youngest graduate had been due to a fire that destroyed some school records many years ago. Nonetheless, it was nice to see her get her photo in the local paper, the *Montgomery Advertiser*.

Serennah did get accepted into the Philadelphia College of Osteopathic Medicine's Georgia campus in their master's program for microbiology. The idea was that if you did well in the master's program you would get a chance to interview for their medical school. She traveled to interviews at DO schools in Virginia, Kentucky, Arizona, and Missouri and got several acceptances. She cried with each unprecedented positive letter and soul-searched to make a final decision on where to attend school. She chose to go to a DO school in Georgia and turned down the other four offers. It was an amazing testament to the talent people saw in her. God orchestrated a place for her to stay with Kip's cousins during her first year away from home at the age of seventeen. We were so thankful for that. No more feeling guilty that we were letting our kids move out too soon. Her initial disappointment had now turned to tremendous joy. She was even chosen to be the class chair, representing her class in meetings with the university staff.

Serennah loves being able to make a difference when she can. I (Mona Lisa) hardly ever volunteer for any extra work, but Serennah is always trying to improve things wherever she can. On one occasion, she opened her mouth at one of these class leadership meetings and made a suggestion to improve the national medical student conference. The next thing you know she had formed a committee and started researching a project. It eventually turned out to be so good that the university paid to send her and a friend to Washington, DC, and Baltimore to speak on enhancing medical student conferences. They also sent her to a San Francisco conference where she and another student delivered a poster presentation on the work they did in Peru on a medical mission service trip.

In August of 2009, Serennah accepted a military scholarship and was commissioned as an ensign in the U.S. Navy at the age of eighteen. The recruiter had to get special permission to sign her on because there is a rule about having to be nineteen. God knew how expensive medical school was and as always He provided. She passed her first board exams and was a little closer to home for her third- and fourth-year rotations in the Birmingham hospital system. She had really wanted to go to Birmingham as an Alabama University med student, but now she found she would achieve her dream of studying in and around those hospitals as an osteopathic student. This was more in line with her beliefs about how patients should be treated anyway.

She now keeps a set of Kip's miniature air force wings pinned on the inside of her white medical coat. She proudly wore the wings inside her dress whites at her graduation from her summer training in Rhode Island in July of 2010.

Serennah is now stationed for a while as a navy doctor in Bethesda, Maryland, and doing her residency. She is driven by the strong calling that she feels in her life. She strives to be a good physician. She looks forward to serving her patients. I know that God is going to use her in a mighty way for His purpose. I sincerely believe this about each of our children. I learned from the life-changing book *A Full*

Quiver by Rick and Jan Hess that when we limit the number of kids that we have, we could be missing out on the next Mozart or the next Billy Graham or the next Harding child. This is a great disaster that has come upon families and potential families around the world. Instead of beautiful, thriving, bountiful households, people settle for smaller visions, short-term results, and simpler expectations. We all need to trust in God's Word more. He did not say, "Be fruitful and divide," nor "subtract," nor even "add," but "Be fruitful and multiply (Genesis 1:22)."

From the Kids

Food Is For . . .
by Heath and Keith (written when they were young)

Food is for growing and not for throwing.
Food is for snacking and not for attacking.
Food is for enjoying and not for destroying.
Food is for eating and not for kneading.
Food is for baking and not for shaking.
But this is the most important thing food is for.
Food is for sharing and not for wearing.

A Fox and an Ox
by Heath and Keith

There once was a fox and an ox that lived in a box.
They had the chickenpox.
They scratched and scratched with all their might.
But it didn't go away until that night.
The next morning the ox had toast with jam.
And the fox had eggs and ham.
And they lived happily ever after with lots of laughter.

The beauty of having kids write poetry is it opens their minds to what they can do. They learn to use the thesaurus, to think about sentence structure, to see words as art and verbal thoughts as providing visual clarity. Their smiles and delight when they listen to you approve of their work are so much fun.

9

The Rest of the Bunch

Listen, my son, to your father's instruction and do not forsake your
mother's teaching. They are a garland to grace your head and a
chain to adorn your neck.

—PROVERBS 1:8–9

Sometimes, holding a child back can unmotivate them. We feel this might have happened a bit a few years ago with our first son, Heath, when he was the first child to bring home two C's one semester.

After Kip was laid off and I (Mona Lisa) went back to work, Heath became a huge help in babysitting. Although Kip wasn't working, he was still working on a doctorate degree full-time. Adding to his studies and his babysitting, Heath began working a part-time job. None of our other kids ever had a job while in school. We have always told them that getting good grades and the scholarships that go with the good grades should be their main focus and in some sense is their job. Heath really stepped up to the plate and was eager to get a part-time job at a Chick-fil-A to help put food on the table.

Kip thinks that our delaying Heath from leaving home to go to a film school could have unmotivated him somewhat. He had to study English with a concentration in film studies. We reasoned that this would help him as a producer/director/screenwriter. English was not the most exciting choice for him, but it was what was available close to home. These are some of the challenges we work with and that you will probably face in your homeschooling adventure as well.

Heath would often joke that since his sisters started college by twelve, he would do it sooner. When the air force transferred us to Alabama, Heath was working hard on his high school transcript. But when we were transferred back to California, we were so excited that he would get the chance to take the same California High School Proficiency Exam that Hannah and Rosannah took. However, he took it at the age of ten. Although he did not pass it the first time, he did start taking dual-enrollment college classes at Foothill College that could be added to his high school transcript because he was doing high school–level work.

Around this time, the media began to start taking notice of our children.

Heath became quite the celebrity (for a brief moment). Huntingdon College ran a story on Heath and the phone started to ring off the hook. There were several local television interviews and Heath and Serennah finally did appear on CNN (you can see the video on our website). Our family was portrayed as "the Brainy Bunch"— hence the title of this book! We thought this was pretty funny, but the news reporters usually try to make our kids look like a bunch of geniuses, even though we are so careful to emphasize that it is only because of God's blessings and our commitment to homeschooling that our kids are attending college by twelve. We even had *The Ellen DeGeneres Show* call to have Heath on, then a few hours later Jay Leno's people called! We were so thrilled. We tried to say yes to both but Jay Leno's people made us choose because they were Ellen's competitors. We had to choose Ellen because her people had called first. Well, after many weeks of delays, they lost interest in us and we never got to go on the show.

Hollywood is so fickle. One minute you are hot. The next minute you are not. We appeared on Trinity Broadcasting Network's *Joy in Our Town* and on WSFA's *Alabama Live!* But one of the best things we did get to do was have a nice article printed in Mary Pride's magazine, *Practical Homeschooling*. A few months later, Hannah was in the paper and on television as "Auburn University's youngest instructor." Then in the fall of 2008 we had a camera crew from Peacock Productions (a subsidiary of NBC) come into our home for a couple of days to get some footage for a potential reality TV series. They pitched the "sizzle reel" to TLC but they were more interested in making money from Jon and Kate Gosselin's sad circumstances. We shared with them that I did not have a college degree because I had been dedicating myself to homeschooling kids and working part-time while my husband finished his degrees. Our point was that our children were excelling and that most homeschooled kids do well regardless of their parents' level of education. If a mom has dropped out of high school, she can take the CHSPE with her kids instead of just sitting in the parking lot like I did while my kids were taking the exam.

> HOLLYWOOD IS SO FICKLE. ONE MINUTE YOU ARE HOT. THE NEXT MINUTE YOU ARE NOT.

Hollywood may have been looking for geniuses at our house,

but all that they found was a normal homeschooling bunch of kids who were being raised with a Christian worldview and conservative values. We think this story is a lot more relatable since everyone can do it!

Heath was much taller in 2011 as a graduate student than he was as an undergraduate student, yet he still stood out among his fellow students. He looked very young and could not even drive when he first started at Troy. Even though his voice had changed, Heath still surprised people when they learned he had earned a master's degree in computer science. For the most part, Heath's grades had been very good. He had Hannah around to help with the math, Mom helped with the Spanish, and Dad was the best proofreader for English papers. Serennah was great with the sciences and they were able to take music appreciation together back when Heath was much shorter than her. She was very mature about having her little brother around on a college campus. She was never embarrassed by him because she was too busy being proud of him.

Heath was enrolled in Troy University's graduate program pursuing a degree in computer science. He had chosen this as a backup plan until he could move away. We hoped that computer science would somehow continue to motivate Heath to work hard so that his grades didn't suffer.

We have not had to push our kids to study. They have been self-motivated by their dreams. They are learning to set their sights on the next thing that will bring them closer to their goal.

Parents can't put callings like our daughter Serennah's calling to medicine into a child's heart. We can only guide our children on their paths and hope they find something that moves them this deeply. Teach your kids what they need to learn at a young age so that they can meet their goals. It is okay if they change their minds along the way. You just have to really listen to what the kids are telling you and ask God for wisdom. He promises to give us wisdom.

Keith learned how to read by five. He was a good independent learner and has been our only child to have a real interest in music. He found our broken violin in Hannah's closet and convinced her to pay for the repairs. Serennah got her music-major friend from Huntingdon College to come by a couple of times a week and give him lessons. We never were strict about making our kids practice the piano even though we have always had one in the house. I guess we just figured that one of these days a child would take a serious interest in music and then we would have to spend the money on lessons. Well, Keith was serious and we were so glad when he declared that this was it: he wanted to be a music major.

So when he was ten we took on the familiar role of high school counselors and mapped out for him what he had to do to finish up his high school curriculum. He began studying to take the ACT and we watched his determination soar. During this critical time I (Mona Lisa) had to quit my part-time job as a nurse and start working full-time in the evenings. It was a huge challenge trying to balance housework with a houseful, homeschooling, and working. I tried to streamline the schoolwork and started a subscription to an online math tutorial program called TabletClass. It was great for Keith because he could get extra help to go along with what he was doing in his *Saxon Math* textbook. He took the ACT two times before being accepted to Faulkner University just after his eleventh birthday. We got the phone call while in a movie theater. I was so surprised—and happy!—because Kip had not even told me that he and Keith had applied to Faulkner University.

We both drove him to take the placement test and to see his adviser. He let him bypass the "Freshman Experience" class and PE for his first year. This was wise of him. He was allowed to take six units (which was two classes) and ease into college life. We monitored his studying habits closely and went over his syllabus with him to make sure that he could keep up with the college pace. The second semester he chose to take twelve units.

Kip and I always say, "Are you sure you are ready for that many units?" Our kids have always been excited to increase their course load and have sometimes wanted to take up to fifteen units. They are usually trying to sell us on the reasons why they *need* to take more classes. They want to graduate and move on. It is great to watch them take charge of their education.

Keith got straight A's his first year and got two B's in his second year. He started to play the clarinet in the concert band and the marching band. These activities come with scholarships and our home is filled with violin, clarinet, and piano music nightly. It was a blessing to finally have a musical child.

Now Keith is talking about going to graduate programs in other states and it has us concerned, because he will only be fifteen when he graduates from Faulkner University. We are trying to talk him into an online degree or just starting a business. But Kip and I still call these good problems to have. At least we are not having to pick up our kids from the police station for cutting class, taking drugs, or something awful like that.

A year ago, as we watched our sixth child, Seth, running across the lawn with his homemade swords and shield, I worried if he would be ready for college at eleven like his older brothers were. But almost immediately I began to feel guilty for even thinking this. I felt guilty because I have had people comment to me that they would not want their kids to go to college by twelve because they want their kids to just be kids.

Whenever I have these doubts, I have to check my heart. I ask the Lord, "Why are we doing this?" I am quickly reminded that we have been blessed to be able to homeschool. Then I remember that we cannot help but to accelerate our kids. This has become the natural progression in our family, and the children want it, too. We would not even know *how* to hold them back and slow them down. I also wonder how we could justify dragging out their elementary and high school years until they are seventeen or eighteen when it does not even give them or us the results we want.

Thoughts like this give me peace. I realize that Seth is so blessed to be on a college campus. He is not stuck all day in a sixth-grade classroom being raised by his peers. He spends his daytime hours with mature adults who are serious about their education and then comes home in the afternoon to run around the backyard with his siblings. His level of academics really has nothing to do with his "getting to be a kid" or not. As a matter of fact, he is very free to be himself because he is free of peer pressure and the need to fit in. There are no other twelve-year-old boys in his classes that he has to dress like, act like, or impress.

Heath also came to this realization on his own. He felt that starting college at eleven freed him from trying to fit in. People were just nice to him. He did not have to be "cool" so others would like him.

Katrinnah turned ten in March 2013 and one month later she was taking the ACT for the first time. This was actually her first standardized test ever. She was all smiles as we discussed how she needed to raise her hand to use the bathroom. We explained that she could not look around too much during the test in order to avoid raising suspicion that she might be trying to cheat. She was happy that Seth would be in the room with her and we asked him to sit somewhere in front of her so that she would know that he was near.

The last thing we told her as we looked her in the eyes was this:

"Today your score does not matter. We just want you to experience what the test is all about."

We immediately saw that she was somewhat relieved. We knew that this was all part of her education. It was about more than just the score. We were so excited that she could be exposed to such an important test at such a young age. After this day, the ACT would not be so mysterious. In a few weeks, when we got her score report back, we would see where her weaknesses were and we would start to work on them. But this day was just to show her that she could sit for a four-hour exam in a room full of high school kids.

After the exam, the smile on her face was confirmation that we weren't pushing our kids. We're just doing things a little different in our family.

WE'RE JUST DOING THINGS A LITTLE DIF-FERENT IN OUR FAMILY.

Now that we do telephone consultations, this is a very important subject that seems to always come up. We share with people that they do not have to send their scores to colleges until Mom and Dad have seen them first. The ACT can be taken multiple times without penalty, which relieves some of the test anxiety. Also, we recommend that reviewing for the ACT/SAT can be introduced to the child at an early age—around eight or nine in our family. When Kip and I took the SAT in the eighties, it was presented as our "one-time shot" to get into college. We know now that it does not have to be presented this way.

•   •   •

We will keep teaching our children the fundamentals. As we work on their character, we'll teach them to love reading and writing. We will build their math skills daily. If we can instill in them a love for learning, we will not have to worry that they will not be educated. They will spend the rest of their lives educating themselves and their children, too. We will not have to worry about any gaps in their education.

Homeschooling parents could always feel inadequate if they focused on the gaps and what their kids *aren't* doing. Instead, we focus on all the great things our kids *are* doing. We just do our best and it really is good enough.

10

The Brainy Bunch Method (Some Practical Advice)

You should mind your own business and work with your hands,
just as we told you, so that your daily life may win the respect of
outsiders and so that you will not be dependent on anybody.
—I THESSALONIANS 4:11–12

Now that we've covered our story and where our children are at, we'd like to share some of our methods. There is no science or formula to our success. We read that if you postpone formal learning until children are older, between about seven and nine, then they can cover grades one through eight in about a six-month period. That's one way to do it. However, we start by age four and finish high school by twelve, eleven, or in Heath's case, ten years and eleven months.

If we were to boil down our methods, they would look a little something like this:

At age four we teach letters, sounds, easy reader books, and tracing letters. Doing school is so much fun! We hear, "Look at me, I am so big!" Learning to read is the most important first step.

By age six we are teaching borrowing and multiplying, encouraging independent reading of easy books, giving a full page of dictation, and teaching Bible stories.

By age eight the children are learning the Bible truths and are learning to really verbalize them. They start algebra and read real chapter books on historical figures and science books, and they do less dictation and more trying to write on their own.

By age ten they are reading the Bible independently and figuring out what they really believe and why, finishing algebra, starting algebra 2 and geometry (figuring out math problems from the solutions manual), writing essays on real-world issues, and reading real books about history and science (we use some of the big siblings' college textbooks if they are interesting). All along we try to find out what motivates the children and allow them to read and research whatever that may be.

By age twelve they have finished lots of high school–level books on creation science, biblical apologetics, history, secular science (like evolution, so they can hear all the viewpoints), physical sciences, American government, economics, social subjects, and lots of math. If you throw in intense family discussions, lots of family/homeschool group field trips, some sports, church, socializing as a family with people of all ages and cultures, and *love*, you end up with a well-adjusted kid who is ready for a college class or two.

We'll share some suggestions for those starting homeschooling and then give some tips we've learned along the way.

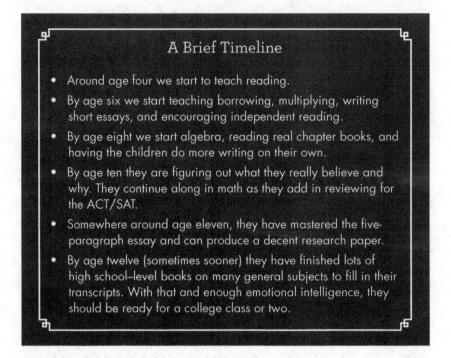

A Brief Timeline

- Around age four we start to teach reading.
- By age six we start teaching borrowing, multiplying, writing short essays, and encouraging independent reading.
- By age eight we start algebra, reading real chapter books, and having the children do more writing on their own.
- By age ten they are figuring out what they really believe and why. They continue along in math as they add in reviewing for the ACT/SAT.
- Somewhere around age eleven, they have mastered the five-paragraph essay and can produce a decent research paper.
- By age twelve (sometimes sooner) they have finished lots of high school–level books on many general subjects to fill in their transcripts. With that and enough emotional intelligence, they should be ready for a college class or two.

Some Suggestions for Starting to Homeschool

Character Building

If we end up with children who are academically brilliant yet have lost their souls, then what have we gained? Nothing. We have failed as parents. So the most important part of our children's education is raising them with a good moral compass. They need to know right from wrong and know why they believe what they believe.

Knowing this, we start off our day with household chores. Each child has assigned chores. As they get older, the easier chores are handed down to the younger ones. This way they grow up feeling needed and knowing that they are a vital part of this family because we really need their help. They won't grow up spoiled because they are developing a good work ethic. Even the two-year-old can spray some water on the fridge and cabinets and have a good time wiping them down and saying, "Look, Mommy, I am a good helper." There won't be any "self-esteem" issues here!

After breakfast and chores, everyone starts with Bible study. Studying God's Word and praying is how we have learned to get through life. I read a Bible story to the younger ones and the older ones read the Bible on their own. This is supplemented with an evening family devotional time that is led by my husband. If I have a really busy day and this is all we get done, well, we've done a lot.

Math

We try to do math after Bible reading because this is where my kids require the most help. And if something comes up, they can always catch up on their reading and writing in a waiting room somewhere or in the car later if necessary.

We started out using Christian Light Publications, then used Alpha Omega Publications (AOP) for math. AOP workbooks go all the way through high school. They are so well written that parents can learn the subjects along with their kids even if the parents feel like they never had the opportunity to learn the material during their own education. Statistically, homeschooled kids do better than the national average regardless of the parents' level of education. After all, it has been said that "education is not the filling of a pail, but the lighting of a fire."

Once the child finishes the third-grade workbooks, we switch to *Saxon Math* textbooks because in the fourth grade kids are usually able to copy problems out of a textbook. We use graph paper to help them get the numbers lined up just right for multiplication and division problems. Eventually, we move on to TabletClass and

KhanAcademy.org (a nonprofit educational website created in 2006 to provide "a free world-class education for anyone anywhere").

English and History

We make sure that our kids write every single day. There are a lot of language arts workbooks and other materials out there. AOP and Christian Light have them, too, but we have come to find that the best way to teach kids to write is to just get them to write. They can choose to write a letter, make an entry in their journal, or staple papers together to make a book they write themselves (they can have fun illustrating these, too!). When they are very young, they can start copying the words and sentences out of their favorite books. They eventually learn how to spell and punctuate this way. As they write on their own, I just proofread as we go, and I explain the grammar rules to them while I make the corrections. They seem to remember them better this way.

After their daily writing, they read and read. They like historical fiction and biographies to learn history, and science books. Their language and writing skills improve the more they read. And I like to do two things at once by having them read history and science books. I don't personally enjoy reading fiction, but some of my kids do. So just like we encourage them in their pursuit of careers, the kids are free to choose to read quality, wholesome books after they finish what I require of them.

This is where some folks say you can homeschool with nothing more than your library card. This is very true. Although I have acquired lots of books over the years, you can get most of what you need from the library. If you want books that are clearly from a Christian worldview, then you may have to find them online or in one of the many, many Christian homeschooling catalogs (e.g. Christian Book Distributors).

Science

Science is fun because it is everywhere. This is the most natural subject to talk about with your kids. Whether you are homeschoolers or "after-schoolers," your kids can start learning about science by just talking to you. Kids will ask questions about their pets, the weather, the bugs that they find, and just about everything else that they see in the physical world around them. We like to give straightforward answers.

Even that dreaded question "Where do babies come from?" gets a straightforward answer: from inside of Mommy. This is good enough at ages three to five. Then the six- or seven-year-old asks, "How does the baby come out?" We proceed with the somewhat graphic answer. "How does the baby get inside of Mommy?" is one of the few questions that Dad has to share all the details of, because Mom likes to delegate this one. But what our kids learn from all of this is that we will *always* tell them the truth . . . even when it comes to the Easter Bunny and Santa Claus.

These discussions, which usually start as you are driving, can lead to research once they get home. For the little guys, a simple trip to the library to check any and every science book of their choosing can open up a whole new world for them. Older kids can learn what the good sites are online to find their own answers to their highly scientific questions. When we cannot give our kids a good answer, they hear, "Ask Heath," "Ask Hannah," or "Text Serennah." Also, "Google it" is a very popular answer. Heath says, "Use DuckDuckGo and Wikipedia."

If these suggestions make you feel uneasy because you need structure, we understand. Feel free to order some boxed curricula that actually have the words on the cover that you are specifically looking for, e.g., "General Science—Ninth Grade," "Biology—Tenth Grade, "Physics—Eleventh Grade." Remember that you can cover lots of science in great detail if your child is very, very interested. We have not actually done any chemistry labs in our kitchen, yet our kids have done very well in their biology, chemistry, and physics labs once they reach the college level. We now know that if they are trained to be good readers and critical thinkers at home, they will do fine in their college-level science courses.

You may decide to just assign general science material, which will cover the basics at a high school level so that their time is freed up to excel in their areas of interest. Just double-check which high school courses are required by the college that your child is planning to attend.

Again, our motto has become "If the kids are happily reading educational material and are being challenged, just get out of their way."

Foreign Languages

The easiest way to bring a foreign language program into your homeschooling is to put the kids in front of the computer with some good language-learning software. Rosetta Stone is probably the most popular, but we hear it is very expensive. We have a small collection of audio CDs and computer software that we have picked up at the base exchange, Walmart, and Target. Because we ask our kids to take Spanish in college, too, we have several college textbooks around the house for the kids who prefer to read the exercises.

We have found that although all of our kids are exposed to the Spanish curriculum, the ones who can actually speak it are the ones who have chosen *on their own* to really practice it. Hannah had to do an intense review on her own so that she could teach Spanish at the private school where she was also teaching math. Rosannah was blessed to marry Sergio from Peru, so now he is her teacher. Serennah signed up to travel abroad on a few medical mission trips and to work as a translator in a medical office while in college. By far, her immersion experiences have helped her become the most fluent. Rosannah is right behind her because of her daily exposure to the language. Heath likes languages in general and studies on his own. He likes to converse with me (I am bilingual) while we prepare supper. Keith and Seth were only mildly interested while they studied Spanish at home, but now that they are taking it in college, they are much more motivated to perform for their professors.

At the high school level, parents can introduce some very basic material, but students can only become fluent if they are inspired to become lifelong learners in the language. Give them opportunities to go into the real world to practice their new language skills. Mine like to study Spanish. We did have an advantage in this area because our home already had the benefit of one parent having been raised in a bilingual home. Knowing more than one language keeps the mind active at any age and opens up a whole new world of cultures and vocabulary.

For all of the other subjects, there is so much we have access to online. Just find out what your child likes, and enjoy this wonderful time in their lives, because they grow up really fast!

Learn by Doing

Hannah, Rosannah, and Serennah learned to read at the private school they briefly attended. I used learning videos to keep Heath occupied occasionally. One day when Heath was four he started to call out the house numbers as he rode in our double stroller behind baby Keith. It occurred to me that if he could recognize the numbers he probably could start to learn the letters, too. So I purchased some flash cards and quickly found that he already knew their names and their sounds. He would say, "I know that, Mommy. I saw that on *Alphabet Friends*." All I had to do was show him that the letters blend together to make words. He was so excited by his newfound knowledge.

As soon as we went to the library, he devoured all of the "easy readers" that they had. It was so much fun trying to keep one step ahead of him. My new job was providing quality reading material for this little sponge. He had so many questions for any of us who would take the time to answer. He shares now that he remembers being frustrated when he could not get the answers that he was looking for from us or in his reading material. He was so thrilled when we finally got Internet access and the world was at his fingertips. He could dive down deep into any area he was curious about.

> IT WAS SO MUCH FUN TRYING TO KEEP ONE STEP AHEAD OF HIM.

I learned a lot from homeschooling him from the very beginning. He was a good example of how kids are naturally curious and able to learn most things on their own if provided with the right tools. I did have to sit next to him to introduce new math concepts. He grasped them rather quickly. Once he learned that Mom would look at the solutions manual when needed, he realized that he was able to do this on his own. At this point, he also found that Hannah knew way more about math than Mom did and Mom was never too proud to refer him to her. She was busy with Keith and Seth at this point anyway and was happy to be out of this job.

Now that we covered the basics for starting to homeschool, here are some helpful tips to guide you:

Don't Be Predictable

Change up what you teach and when you teach. It's all part of the fun and it's actually good for the mind to alternate routines.

Be silly. Be creative. Keep them guessing what you'll do next.

Use the great outdoors as the best classroom possible. If I start to feel bored or burned out, we go on a field trip, a walk, or a playdate with some friends. We know that there is so much learning that goes on just when your kids are talking to you while you visit a museum, you walk around the zoo together, or they interact with kids of different ages and backgrounds. Library visits always give us a new spark because the kids can spend a day just reading. This gives me some quiet time so I can clear my own mind.

I have been known to send a bunch of hyper kids to run around the yard to burn off some steam, especially if the rain has kept us cooped up in the house.

Learning is best done when we teach our kids practical lessons and show them how the real world works. This is where they get their emotional intelligence. Emotional intelligence is defined as the ability to *identify, assess, and control* one's emotions. Children may be academically brilliant and ready to start college very young, but they might break out in tears if the professor hands them a test paper with a big red F on it. We teach our kids that if they ever have something unpleasant happen to them in class (e.g., a bad grade or a rude comment from a classmate), they need to just "keep it together" until they get home. As soon as they get in the car, they can let loose and cry if they need to.

We talk about this enough in our family that our kids know that we will be there to laugh with them and cry with them. The confidence that they are safe at home to express any emotions that they feel helps them to be able to go into the college classroom and do very well emotionally. We teach them that they need to be able to *identify, assess, and control* their emotions while in the classroom. We would not let them start college until we were confident that they were mature enough in this area. Academics are not everything.

> AS SOON AS THEY GET IN THE CAR, THEY CAN LET LOOSE AND CRY IF THEY NEED TO.

Emotional intelligence is closely related to social awareness, which we also deem to be as important as academics. An example of social awareness is the ability to recognize who is least likely to be heard in a group setting and have the empathy and wisdom to speak out about their opinion. We teach our kids to seek out that person in the group who is being left out and try to talk to them. Social awareness is also knowing how to dress, when to speak up, and, more important, when to be quiet.

Everyone Contributes

All for one and one for all, as the saying goes. Everyone, from the adult children to the toddlers, can still contribute. Everyone can play a part. This is how they learn to work as a team and how they will continue to mature and grow.

Eat Together

You may have heard that families who eat together are less likely to have problems down the road with their children. There are many lessons to be learned around the supper table. Make this a priority to help boost the emotional intelligence of your children.

While we often try to eat organic, sometimes as a parent you have to just relax and let the kids make their own dinner. Occasional cereal parties can do wonders.

Mona Lisa Montoya married Kip Harding on December 26, 1986. We were both 18.

This photo is from 1992 at Fort Rucker, AL, where Kip was at his helicopter pilot training. Serennah (1), Hannah (4), and Rosannah (2).

Hannah earns a master's in mathematics at the age of 19 from Cal State East Bay Hayward.

LEFT: This is the photo we used in Rosannah's portfolio when I sent in her application to California College of the Arts (CCA) in San Francisco. She was 15 when she was accepted as a transfer student. She was already a junior in college.

BELOW: May 27, 2005. Mariannah Priscilla, baby #8 is born.

Heath, Hannah, Seth, Rosannah, and Keith at the Grand Canyon.

Heath's first day at Foothill Community College at age 10 1/2. He looks so small!

Rosie's first day at CCA in San Francisco at age 16.

Rosannah graduates at 18 with a BA of Architecture with High Distinction from CCA in Dec. 2007.

Serennah in the newspaper, 2008.

Hannah, Serennah, and Rosannah at Serennah's graduation from Huntingdon College with a BA in Microbiology at the age of 17 in May 2008.

Seth, Heath, and Keith getting some character training in 2005—"speak no evil, see no evil, hear no evil."

Rosannah had the opportunity to meet Colin Powell in 2013 when she was invited as the AIA's youngest member.

Kip reading the story of the first Thanksgiving to the kids in 2007.

Young Keith is playing an educational game on the computer while Katie soaks it all in. There is always learning going on.

Keith, age 13, in band at a football game.

Heath at 17.

Keith with his violin at age 14.

Seth graduated from high school
at age 11.

Kip loves taking the family down
to the beach. This photo depicts his
fathering approach—work hard then
relax hard.

Serennah graduates from Philadelphia College of Osteopathic Medicine at the age of 22.

We had the wonderful opportunity to give a PowerPoint presentation at a Homeschool Expo, and the kids enjoyed answering FAQs at the booth. We offered our ebook and consulting.

Rosannah's birthday was in the summer so she could never take cupcakes to share with her classmates. So we made up "Half-Birthdays." We are always looking for a reason to celebrate and bake something sweet! The photo is of Lorennah at 5 1/2.

Thunder James, born
March 28, 2010.

Kip got to escort Serennah
to her formal dinner when
she graduated from medical
school. (May 2013)

The whole family, May 2013.

Lessons at the Dinner Table

Dinner table discussions usually start with Dad saying, "Hey, kids, you will never guess what I heard on the radio driving home today . . ." These discussions can be about the latest technological advances, like Google Glass or India's next mission to Mars, or something that the kids learned in class on any given day. We allow our kids to share their thoughts and ideas and try to ask them lots of questions to stimulate critical thinking.

Field Trips Are Great!

Another way to break up the routine while learning is to schedule field trips. Trips to places like the zoo are ideal outings. They're fun but also educational. The kids can write a paper on the experience or simply make journal entries about the trip.

Exercise Your Body to Exercise Your Spirit

We love to walk as a family and focus not just on our minds but on our bodies. Our kids love participating in the Awana program. Awana (the name comes from the first letters of Approved Workmen Are Not Ashamed, from 2 Timothy 2:15) is an international evangelical nonprofit organization kind of like the Boy or Girl Scouts. Their website is Awana.org.

WE LOVE TO WALK AS A FAMILY AND FOCUS NOT JUST ON OUR MINDS BUT ON OUR BODIES.

Pamper Yourself

Go ahead and spoil yourself every now and then. Don't expect things to go right all the time. But when they do, celebrate the small successes. Treat yourselves to rewards. Not just rewards for the children but for you.

Remember: success is measured in moments, not at the end of the race.

Serve Together

We love helping out as a family in doing things like tornado recovery and other service-oriented projects. This allows us to give back while also helping the children see other parts of the world and realize how vital it is to help others in need.

Serving in something like the Kid's Club is a great opportunity to share the gospel in a public setting. Kid's Club was sponsored by our nondenominational Christian church. Hannah went with a group into public elementary schools to share Bible stories, songs, games, crafts, and snacks after school hours. Attendance was voluntary and parents had to give written consent. These clubs were very popular in the Sunnyvale area because parents and teachers were seeing how the teachings were helping the kids become better behaved during their daytime classes. Check for something similar in your area.

Family Time

We always carve out family time. Whether we're at a pool or a zoo or outdoors playing, our family time is always quality time.

Teach Them About Life

Limit how much time your children watch mindless television. There are positive shows that can be watched. Just mute the bad commercials or quickly change the channel when necessary. The kids like to watch TLC's *19 Kids and Counting* with Mom. They know that Dad will usually be watching the news, the Military Channel, the History Channel, or a science program on the Discovery Channel. They are free to sit and watch if they are interested. But they have to hold their questions until there is a commercial or else we cannot keep up with them. One question always seems to lead to more questions. There is usually someone on the computer, as we are watching the program, looking up all of those answers that Mom and Dad cannot give. When watching educational TV, talk to your kids about what they see.

Movies based on true stories that have an object lesson can teach your children about the crazy world we live in (so that nothing in college will shock them). Discuss current events around the dinner table, treating them as adults in the conversation.

Studying the book of Proverbs will give them more of the emotional intelligence and wisdom that they will need to interact with adults.

Make sure to teach your children social skills. You don't want the stereotypical "nerdy" or insulated homeschoolers in your house.

Dare to Dream!

We are thankful that our kids have been able to develop their God-given talents. We see the irony in so many things, like Rosannah growing up to study architecture, where the "doodling" that she was once scolded for is a way of life and is constantly encouraged. Too many children lose their passion for learning when they are stuck in a public school setting.

Feeling Unqualified?

Worried because you don't have a college degree? Children can become well educated regardless of whether or not you have one. Although I (Mona Lisa) had been accepted to Santa Clara University, I decided to marry my high school sweetheart and be a mom instead. In the past, I never felt the need to finish my college degree since I started down the path of marriage and family. Perhaps when Thunder is twelve and I am fifty-four, I will finish college with him. Who knows? We will see.

When Opposed, Stick Together

There will be plenty of people who do not understand what you are doing nor why you are doing it. There will be doubters and cynics. Just like when Heath's professor said that he didn't have enough life experience to write, and we encouraged Heath with the story of young Anne Frank.

Know that you'll face opposition, but you and your kids can work through it together if you're really determined to use our method.

Socialization Ideas

Looking for ideas?
Ask your kids!

- Who wants to take a dance class?
- Who wants to join 4-H?
- Who wants to go to the hobby store and try their hand at painting?
- Who wants to play their instrument and/or sing at the local nursing home?

Work Smarter, Not Harder

We have friends who pay for a few high school classes at local schools even though they mostly homeschool their kids. The classes can be very challenging and very expensive. We could never understand why someone would want to go this route. We suspect that the kids convince their parents to allow them to go so they can be with kids their age.

We understand that this type of socialization is important to teenagers. There are plenty of other opportunities for kids to interact with others their age (see sidebar). Check your local network for more ideas, too. These kids could be working smarter by pouring their energy into course work that will earn them college credit as they simultaneously finish up high school.

We realize that in some households kids are allowed to simply make their own decisions. We like to help our kids make *well-informed* choices. Our kids see the logic in working smarter, not just harder. Parents can get the vision first and then pass that vision on to their kids. Confidence can be contagious.

CONFIDENCE CAN BE CONTAGIOUS.

From the Kids

Serennah's Personal View of Homeschooling
[2011]

If my parents ever learned to model their parenting after a wise source, they did so by modeling after God. Every parent faces a challenge when they have more than one child: the unique challenge of loving all entirely but each one entirely as well. My mother says they do this by loving the one who needs them the most at any given moment. This is true. I'd like to think also, though, that my parents modeled this principle of God's as well: they love each of their children the same amount. But they love each of their children differently.

In the same manner, when it comes to fostering our educations, my parents recognize that each of us has unique talents. Each of us has different passions that must be "loved" differently. So here are some unique highlights of my story.

I'll never forget the day I walked down our home stairway to chat with my parents about my calling. I was thrilled to announce I had made a sure decision. I wanted to study science. I wanted to study medicine. I wanted to become a doctor. Who gave me that idea? It kind of just came. Ever since I was little, I had no particular interest. I never declared one passion or goal. But when the time came that I was supposed to make my decision . . . it felt as if it had already been made. I was supposed to become a doctor. I had been created to be a doctor. I really believed that. I still do to this day.

I am so very humbled to be able to serve my patients now that I am a doctor. I know that it is a huge responsibility and I do not take it lightly. I will show my gratitude to my God, my family, and my country by working hard and being the best doctor that I can be.

Every single day since I was eleven, since that day I talked with my parents, I have learned how much I didn't know then. I didn't know what it was going to take. I didn't know what being a doctor really meant. I didn't know the meaning of a "long, hard day." But I did know I had made a decision. I did know I had been given a passion. I did know I had parents ready to kindle what I brought to the table.

My pursuit of becoming a doctor started that day in our living room. And since deciding that, I've learned some big lessons in the last year and a half.

My father once told me, "Shoot for the stars, and you just might land on the moon." He also once told me to "aim for the greatest contribution [I] can make in this world." Aim for the greatest contribution? Hmm . . . greatest contribution? Well, God will be the judge of that. But I can start somewhere.

Perhaps my mother has shared the specifics with you about my story. I sat down tonight to write them out, but I think I will spare the details and continue the story. It was such a pleasure to be in medical school . . . pleasure? Say what? It truly was the most fun thing you never want to do again. Here's a look at my diary at the time:

> It's 7:30 pm on a Saturday night. I am writing from a study room on my campus. I arrived here at 8:30 this morning. The white board behind me contains a scratch of my thoughts when I walked in this morning, "Aim for the Greatest Contribution you can make in this world." I plan to leave the writing there for when I leave later tonight so that the next student who uses

this room will study with the same charge that I did today. I have 39 hours of lecture to work through. 92 questions to work through in a question bank, and 4 sets of 15 questions from my board review program to work through. All before Monday at 5 am when my alarm goes off to start next week. I will do what I can. We have suturing clinic, scrub and hospital day this week. I will pick this up soon . . .

Today is April 30th, 2011. Yesterday, I just completed my first 2 years of my medical school training. When a goal becomes in closer reach, I always like to reflect on the past and how I got to where I am. All the praise goes to God. He gives me the strength and the ability. I give Him the persevering spirit. This resonated with me today . . . perhaps it will speak to you, too.

Harvey Mackey wrote the following notes for the entrepreneur section of an article collection:

To simply ask the question, "How can I make a difference?" is to answer it, because the answer is to never let yourself stop asking the question. I've asked myself that question hundreds of times. And any time I feel like quitting, I just look at a framed poster I have hanging in our office:

- He failed in business in '31.
- He ran as a state legislator and lost in '32.
- He tried business again in '33 and failed again.
- His sweetheart died in '35.
- He had a nervous breakdown in '36.
- He ran for state elector in '40 after he regained his health.
- He was defeated for Congress in '43, defeated again for Congress in '48, defeated when he ran for Senate in '55 and defeated for vice presidency of the United States in '56.

- *He ran for Senate again in '58 and lost.*
- *This man never quit. He kept trying till the last.*

    In 1860, this man—Abraham Lincoln—was elected president of the United States.

    I want to be like Abe Lincoln. As my dad always says, "Shoot for the stars, and you just might land on the moon." I am aiming to make my greatest contribution in this world. I don't need easy. I just need possible. *And thanks to God, there are no* impossibles *with Him. That is a big idea.*

From the Kids

Heath's Personal View of Homeschooling
[2013]

According to my mom, I was one of the youngest babies who talked, even between my mom nursing me. I went from being weaned to watching all things educational when my baby brother was born. My earliest memory is of watching the videos called *Alphabet Friends*. I remember always being able to read well. I read all of the signs along the central California highways from Vandenberg AFB to Silicon Valley. Before my family moved from California (where my first memories began), I remember reading on the grass while my oldest sister attended college classes. My mom would walk a stroller around the campus track so she could be nearby. I remember asking my mother thousands of questions about every subject that popped into my head. Because we had such a small class size (as homeschoolers) she had plenty of time to answer each question to the best of her abilities. As I got older, my interest shifted from the television to our new computer. One of my favorite activities was playing educational computer games. I remember discovering how odd it was that someone at my age (six or seven) was beating games intended for sixth graders. My first college class was Intermediate Algebra at Foothill College in California. I remember befriending two high schoolers who were dually enrolled there and were quite surprised that my grades were much higher than theirs. The next semester I took a statistics class and an introductory composition class at the age of eleven. I remember working with two thirty-year-olds on a statistics project and getting my first

B grade in the English class. Thinking back to that first English class, I am surprised that I chose to major in the subject if I was clearly doing much better in the other more left-brained classes.

I was excited about getting a digital arts degree at Foothill, but my parents let me know that we were going to move back to Alabama after my semester was over, so we looked for similar degrees in Montgomery. When I started at Huntingdon, I planned on studying for a theater degree because of my interest in acting. Huntingdon offered a concentration in film studies for their English major. After I was able to finish that degree in 2011, I went back to my first passion and began to study computer science at Troy University. In May of 2013, I completed that degree also. So I now possess a BA in English and an MS in computer science.

11

From Mom to Mom—
Keeping It All Together

Rejoice in the Lord always. I will say it again: Rejoice! Let your
graciousness be known to everyone. The Lord is near. Don't worry
about anything, but in everything, through prayer and petition
with thanksgiving, let your requests be made known to God. And
the peace of God, which surpasses every thought, will guard your
hearts and minds in Christ Jesus.
—PHILIPPIANS 4:4–7

I (Mona Lisa) am a list maker. I feel that if I write it down, it will get done—well . . . eventually. Many times priorities change and things get crossed off the list or just moved over to another list. Having this helpful map of the day and directions for what needs to happen allows me to check off the important details. And there are certainly lots of them!

Organized Chaos

People always comment, "So you must have a strict schedule to get it all done." I am usually very tongue-tied trying to explain that we really don't have a schedule. It is more like a to-do list for each child. We get up as early as we can (depending on what we were doing as a family the night before) and then work to reach some simple goals:

1. Clean rooms, get dressed.
2. Eat breakfast.
3. Comb hair, brush teeth.
4. Chores (dishes, trash, pick up stuff around house, feed and water dog, clean table, etc.). Each kid does the same chores every day. Changes are made as they get older.
5. Start school with Bible reading, because we know that the fear of the Lord is the beginning of wisdom. We are teaching our kids that their character development is the most important part of their education.
6. Mathematics. We do this second every day because it is incremental and shouldn't be skipped if the day gets crazy.
7. They need to write every day—a letter, an essay, a journal entry, a page of dictation, etc. . . .
8. Lots of reading—biographies, historical fiction, science books. Then they can read fiction for fun. (I.e., quality literature like *The Chronicles of Narnia* or *The Boxcar Children* during the early years. See some suggestions at the end of this book.)
9. PE, which over the years has included: jumping on the trampoline, family walks, hikes, Victory sports league (our local Christian homeschool sports organization), soccer, playing Ultimate Frisbee with a local group, or just riding bikes on our property.

A Sample Schedule

We follow more of a checklist than a timed schedule. The kids are free to do things in the order that inspires them. Sometimes they really get into a subject and will postpone a few subjects for another day. We are flexible and even let them make substitutions (such as geography for Spanish) for a time as long as we know there is learning going on.

This is taped to our front door:

Katrinnah's Schedule:

- Get dressed
- Eat breakfast
- Chores
- Bible study
- ACT review (a section a day)
- Writing
- Lunch
- Reading (history and science)
- Math (if not covered in the ACT review)
- Spanish
- Violin or piano (they alternate)
- 2:30, ready or not, PLAY OUTSIDE!
- no homework "allowed" in the evenings—just reading for fun

The Morning Rush

"Good morning, sunshine!" This is how my little ones are greeted in the morning one by one. There is no morning rush to get dressed, eat breakfast, pack the lunches, finish last-minute homework, load up the car, and fight traffic to drop off kids at school. Homeschoolers can have peace in the morning instead of the mad rat race to get everyone to school on time.

It feels so much more natural for the younger children to wake up when their bodies are ready. Lorennah, our five-year-old, sleeps in the longest. She is a petite little thing and the kids decided that we should let her sleep in so she will grow to her fullest potential. Thunder is three and is the first one to wake up most mornings, asking for cereal. My college kids set their own alarms. They know what their study schedules should be. I don't need to keep track of them. I just need to know who needs a ride.

HOMESCHOOL-
ERS CAN HAVE
PEACE IN THE
MORNING IN-
STEAD OF THE
MAD RAT RACE
TO GET EVERY-
ONE TO SCHOOL
ON TIME.

I get to enjoy the quiet of the morning as the children wake up one by one. If the kids are not feeling well, they can stay in bed. Once they get bored, they can start reading in bed or watching some educational videos. So we don't have a problem with sick days. I remember when my older girls were in a private school during flu season and how I always felt pressured to send them back to school even though they weren't fully recovered. This wasn't good for them or the poor kids they were infecting. We don't have this pressure anymore. As a matter of fact, when my kids came down with the chicken pox at our house, it was just another day. Once we got the itching under control, they could read, rest, and play educational games. There were no worries about how many days they were "missing" from school.

When you fill out a home-school affidavit in California, you must list your school name. A good friend of mine joked about how she was going to call hers the Nanny Nanny Boo Boo School. She explained that on those freezing-cold mornings when her kids curl up on the couch, under the blankets, drinking their hot cocoa, waiting to start their family devotions, they see the poor kids walking to the bus stop, and they say "nanny nanny boo boo" through the window because they get to stay home. Although this may sound a little mean-spirited, many homeschoolers pray for their peers at public schools. We are now losing successive generations of people in America to minds and lives without the beneficial knowledge and foundation of Christ.

Believing in Homeschooling and Your Children

Have you ever seen the bumper sticker "A bad day fishing is better than a good day at work"? This is how we feel about keeping your kids at home with you. I (Mona Lisa) have had those days where I think that it did not go well and there were so many interruptions that things did not go as planned.

For example, one day we were driving the boys to class and then on the way home our van broke down and we "wasted" a couple of hours on the side of the road waiting for a tow truck. During that time, some of the kids were reading in the van while the rest of us just talked. We gave thanks to God that we broke down in a nice shady spot and that we were safe. The time spent waiting for the tow truck turned out to be nice bonding time. Yes, they could have been in a classroom somewhere learning random facts that they would soon forget. Thankfully, they were with me and with each other. So, even when things do not go exactly as planned, my kids are better off being with me.

So, my dear new homeschoolers, trust in Deuteronomy 6, where we are told to teach our children the truth as we walk down the path of life (or sit on the side of the road). Your children's being instructed by you, the one who loves and knows your children the most, is far better than being in a crowded classroom and taught by an over-worked teacher who cannot give them the individual attention that they need.

Believing that you are called to homeschool is half the battle. Figuring out what curriculum to use can be the fun part if you let your kids help you. We do not believe that there is a *magic* curriculum. It is more important that your kids enjoy it and are challenged. Skip through the easy parts and spend more time where it is needed. Talk to your kids about their interests and browse with them online and/ or at the library. If your child wants to be president of the United States, design his or her curriculum around what you (the parents) believe is important for a good president to know. Believe that your child *really* can become the president someday. Your confidence will give your child confidence.

To follow that example, if my child wanted to be president and could not read yet, I would read them biographies of some good presidents. If the child could read, I would allow them to read independently about our past presidents. As the child got older, I would start introducing political science, history, law, and government books. Most important, I would want my child to know the book of Proverbs well so that they could be as wise as the wisest leader in history: King Solomon. The child could write every day about what they are reading. Add in math, science, and any electives that interest your child and you have a full curriculum. It doesn't matter if your child is little Prince George of England or a pauper (as in Disney's *The Prince and the Pauper*); we all share interests and need opportunities to explore them. Children have desires that can only be fulfilled if they are allowed the opportunity. The course work could look a little different if you have a musician or an artist in your family. The beauty of homeschooling is that you have the freedom to give your child *exactly* what they need—no more and no less.

From the Kids

Keith's Personal View of Homeschooling
(written at age 11)
[2009]

I have had many life changing experiences, and I believe almost everyone has. The effects of death, marriage, and addictions can cause big changes in a person's life. Some people try to force change in their lives, but most change in a person's life comes naturally. I feel natural change is the best kind of change, because it is destined by God. One of the biggest changes in my life was when I went from being a homeschooler to a college student.

One change that affected me was my sleeping time. Most days I woke up at 8 a.m., because I did not have to be driven to school. On weekdays, my family probably had breakfast around 9 a.m. and started school at 9:30 a.m. College is a big switch from homeschooling. I have a 7 a.m. class this semester, so I have to wake up at 5:30 a.m. to get dressed, eat breakfast, and drive to school. My average bedtime was affected, too. When I was homeschooled I got 11 hours of sleep most nights. Now, I probably go to sleep at 10 p.m. most nights because of homework, so that only allows me 7.5 to 8 hours of sleep. That is more sleep than most students get, but it was a change for me.

Another change that affected me was the driving time each day. Obviously, I did not have to drive to school as a homeschooler, but now, I have a thirty-minute drive every day. My parents are very busy, so sometimes it is a hassle to drop me off and pick me up every day. My mom has to load up all my younger siblings with their reading materials to come pick me up from school.

My homeschooling work was easier than college work. I am studying more subjects now than I did when I was homeschooled like Bible and Music Theory, and the more classes I have make the semester harder. When I was homeschooled, I received one-on-one attention in every subject. Now, in college there are multiple students in every class, which sometimes makes it harder to get my questions answered.

Overall, college and homeschooling are very different. Although college has its share of stress, I think having the experiences of both homeschooling and college has made me a stronger person. I believe the changes have made me a better person.

12

A Day in the Life of a Thirteen-Year-Old Sophomore in College

You have decided the length of our lives. You know how many
months we will live, and we are not given a minute longer.

—JOB 14:5

I (Mona Lisa) wrote this four years ago when Heath was thirteen years old. (2008)

6:00 a.m.—Wake-up time. Heath has breakfast on his own, unless I have some free time to cook breakfast (it's usually only on birthdays that we have a very special breakfast). He usually eats a bagel or some toast. If he wakes up late, he just runs out the door while his dad is honking because it is now seven and Dad is late for work. Heath gets dropped off at school two miles down the road.

7:10 a.m.—Heath can be found in class conversing with students about anything and everything. Many times he has to explain how

131

he got there so young. They have funny names for him such as "boy genius." The big football players call him "big man" and some of the shorter soccer players pay him respect as well.

8:00 a.m.—Class starts. On Wednesday the 10th, Heath finishes up the fall semester. He took calculus, Spanish, world religions, and American literature. He has gotten all A's the past two semesters. He may get a B in calculus and in Spanish. We will soon see. On Jan. 12th, the new semester starts. He is taking five courses because I think he has way too much free time. He is scheduled to graduate in May of 2011 at the age of fifteen. He will be breaking his sisters' records. They graduated at seventeen. Next semester, he will be taking Effective Public Communication, Wisdom and Poetic Literature, British Lit. II, Spanish II, and Media and Society. Public speaking will be a big deal for him.

9:00 a.m.—Heath can be found walking across campus. EVERYONE smiles at him and he waves. I am sure they think, "There is that little kid."

10:30 a.m.—Class is over and Heath has to find Chelly, the eighteen-year-old friend of one of our daughters who gives him a ride home because he is too young to drive. She drops him off and comes over a couple of days a week to give my ten-year-old his violin lesson.

10:45 a.m.—Heath gets home and is STARVING. Again, he has to feed himself and any littler ones who are hanging around the kitchen because lunchtime in our house means "every man for himself," except that older children should always help out their younger siblings.

11:30 a.m.—After Heath shares his day with us, I tell him to go "do something constructive." I trust him to prioritize his time, though I do have to check on him frequently because he gets easily distracted. I really think that if he were in a "regular" school he would get into trouble for talking and joking around too much with the other kids. I am glad that he is around more mature students during the day. He does his chores, such as cleaning his room, doing his own laundry (I do not do this for the big kids, either), and sweeping the kitchen. If he has a test coming up or a big assignment, I give him the space to get it done. If he has some free time, I get him to help me by watching the baby. He also listens to his five-year-old sister read out loud, helps his eight-year-old brother with his algebra, or proofreads his ten-year-old brother's page of dictation. Sometimes, I just need him to keep the peace by keeping the three-year-old happy. I know that he is learning crowd control and people skills that will help him in his future.

Some afternoons Heath tutors a fourteen-year-old girl in algebra. He also tutors high school, homeschooled students in algebra. Heath will occasionally go over to help a couple of elderly women with some basic software applications. He may have a Math Club meeting on a Thursday night, but he has not been allowed to do many extra-curricular activities by the college's administration.

Heath is really excited about being able to get involved in the theater. I will be contacting the administration about opening this up to him this January (2009) and allowing him to start participating in that department since his major is English with a concentration in film studies. He would like to be involved in putting on a production more than just the acting. This is his passion. You should see his eyes light up when he talks about the kind of movies he would like to make someday.

In the evenings, we mostly hang out as a family. Our kids are each other's best friends. Our most favorite thing to do is watch a movie as a family. We like to watch the classics, not just the latest movies. Heath is really interested in how movies are made and he loves to memorize dialogue.

A couple of weeks ago, a family friend took Heath and his sister to the Montgomery Symphony. He has been to many plays, ballets, musical events, Christian concerts, and museums with mom and dad, his sisters, other relatives, and friends of the family.

Our kids have been exposed to much more than just hanging out at the mall with friends who are the same age and dress and talk the same way. Being a military family, they have lived in many different states and have met lots of different kinds of people. Heath does get to interact with kids his age at church and during soccer season, but he is not "peer dependent."

Birthdays at our house are very special. We don't usually invite anyone over for most birthdays. We tell the kids that they will get more presents if we do not have to feed lots of people. But the big birthdays are quinceañeras (fifteenth-birthday Mexican celebrations for our girls), eighteenth birthdays, and twenty-first birthdays. We have been known to throw some BIG birthday bashes in the backyard where we invite everyone we know. We also do this for graduations. Our family loves to eat and we love to dance! You should see Heath dance. He turned thirteen on Nov. 11th, Veteran's Day.

Weekends at our house are all about catching up on homework and then relaxing. We may even do some home improvement projects where everyone pitches in, then we will go for a walk or out somewhere. It is usually with the family. If Kip and I go out alone for a date, Heath is happy to watch his younger siblings with his sisters. This is their excuse to have a "kid party." I do not know exactly what goes on at these "kid parties" because I have never been invited.

Vacations for a while were limited to PCS-ing. This stands for Permanent Change of Station. Which, when we were a military family, meant moving every three years. This is why our kids have gotten to see parts of Kansas, Colorado, Utah, Nevada, California, New Mexico, Arizona, Texas, Mississippi, Louisiana, Alabama, and Georgia. We have been to Disney World, Disneyland, camping in Yosemite, hiking in the Grand Canyon, visiting the hotels of Las Vegas, watching the Oakland A's play baseball, visiting Hearst Castle, boogie-boarding at Pismo Beach, sightseeing in San Francisco, skiing at Lake Tahoe, and enjoying Dusty Millers at a private country club in New Jersey. Most of these events were made possible because of military moves.

From the Kids

Seth's Personal View of Homeschooling
[2013]

The farthest back I can remember is learning how to read. I was five and I absolutely hated reading. I disliked it so much that I was actually trying to figure out which job would not require reading. As soon as I could read well, I got in trouble for reading when I was supposed to be doing other subjects. We are encouraged to read all we want, but in the morning we have to do things in order. We do our chores first, Bible study, math, writing, then we can read for history and science. After all this, we are free to read just for pleasure. Now I cannot imagine life without books, especially history books. My favorite history books are the ones on the medieval ages. I do not remember what sparked my interest in the medieval ages but I do remember that when I got my first library card that was the *only* subject I wanted to read about. After seeing all the amazing pictures, it was my goal to make every type of medieval weapon possible (I had already made a couple). I remember the look on my mother's half-amazed, half-terrified face as I brought out a *huge* fully functional crossbow.

By age eleven, I had made several medieval costumes. During this time, I took the ACT and got a 17. I was accepted conditionally to Faulkner University, where Keith was already attending. Their standard is 18 but I am so glad they gave me a chance. I was able to take the exam again later when Katrinnah took it for the first time to "keep her company," as my mother says. I got a 21 this time. I decided to major in history and eventually transferred to Huntingdon College, just down the street from our house. I am now able to walk home from class if Mom is busy with the younger kids. I carry my university ID just in case a police officer ever stops me to ask why I am not in school. I wonder if the officer would even believe me?

Serennah and Heath graduated from Huntingdon and I am looking forward to graduating from there, too, hopefully by my fifteenth birthday if all goes well.

13

Tips for Non-Homeschooling Parents

"His master replied, 'Well done, good and faithful servant! You have been faithful with a few things; I will put you in charge of many things. Come and share your master's happiness!'"
—MATTHEW 25:21

We realize that there are some readers who are curious about our family's method yet aren't homeschooling. So can you apply these principles to your kids? What advice and input can we share with you?

Here are some tips for those of you who don't homeschool.

1. Character building is still at the top of our list because kids must learn the golden rule: "Therefore all things whatsoever ye would that men should do to you, do ye even so to them: for this is the law and the prophets" (Matthew 7:12). As Christians we rely on the Bible as a reference and guide. It is up to each parent to decide what values they want to instill in their kids.

2. Parents should be aware of what their kids are learning in school. This goes back to being responsible for what values their kids are learning. If the material is objectionable, the parents may have to take it to the schoolteacher, the principal, or even the school board and try to opt out of the days where that material is being taught. Sometimes the administration listens. If the battle is lost, it may be best for your child to leave the school.

3. Take the time to know who your child's friends are. They need to "love their neighbor" but they do not need to imitate negative behaviors. This goes back to character building. They need to know why they believe what they believe. If their classmates are up to no good, your child needs to be careful to associate with them as little as possible.

4. Personally, we are completely against homework because kids should be getting plenty of academics in the seven or so hours that they have been in school. Kids absolutely benefit from family time in the evenings and on weekends. Helping your kids with their homework will help them get it over with so that they are free to spend quality time with you. Encourage them to get it done while at school during any downtime that they may have, if possible. Ask the school to schedule free periods for your child.

5. Try to eliminate homework as much as you can. If your child's teacher keeps sending home "busy work" (lots of work sheets with too many of the same problems), maybe at your next teacher's conference you can suggest a way for your child to show proficiency in that area (like testing out) so that your child will not be required to spend valuable family time on repetitive work sheets.

6. If your child shows that they may be gifted, do all you can to ensure that they are placed in a gifted program or allowed to skip a grade. Switching to a magnet school, charter school, or a private school in your area may enable your child to stay challenged and not get bored. Also look into a tutor provided by the school or locally in order to get that essential one-on-one time.

7. If you must work, you might be able to find someone in your area to homeschool your child for pay. Think of all the money you would save (if you are paying tuition per year) if your child ended up graduating early! Check with the Home School Legal Defense Association (HSLDA.org) to see if the laws in your state will allow this.

8. Some might be expecting us to write about ways to supplement the curriculum and *add* more for your kids to do. We really feel bad about kids having to be away from their families all day and so we do not think that they need any more busy work. But if you must supplement, let your child choose what they want to learn about by finding their specific interests like we discussed earlier. Schools dictate what kids have to learn all day. You, on the other hand, can inspire learning at home by *allowing* your kids to pursue their interests. This should not be forced.

9. Look for ways for your child to graduate early by taking extra credits or skipping a grade. Also prepare them for the ACT and/or the SAT. Allow them to take it early so that the mystery is eliminated and you can improve over a number of years rather than a mad, stressful rush to do it junior/senior year of high school. You may be surprised to see their score. If they do well, you might be inspired to let them dual-enroll at a local college. If your child is really unhappy at their high school, you might even let them take the

GED (which they can do at sixteen in many states) and just start college early.

10. Plan projects that teach something. A really fun project parents can do with their kids is to build a deck. I have had a great time working with my kids on my deck. They learned a whole lot of skills and you get to learn along with them. You can watch YouTube videos and read websites together and take fun road trips to buy wood and stop for ice cream. It really can be a special bonding time if your child takes interest. However, don't start a massive project if it doesn't appeal to them or they won't benefit from it.

Tips for Non-Homeschoolers

1. Help your child see the connection between what they are learning in school and how it may help them in their career in the future.
2. Help your child free up some time to explore their own interests.
3. Help your child become self-sufficient in their own education.
4. Help your child come up with a realistic plan of how to meet their career goals.
5. Help your child to learn to interact with others outside their own age group.
6. Help your child to *dream big* by not falling short of their full potential. For example, don't just try to become a chef but aim for owning a restaurant!

From the Kids

Katrinnah's Personal View of Homeschooling
[2011]

I was born March 12. My favorite subject is math and science. I only like math when I understand it. I like science because science experiments are very fun. I am 8 years old and I am learning algebra. I am interested in dancing at this point in time. My brother took the ACT this summer he is ten and I am going to take the test next. My favorite thing to do is draw pictures for my dad. He says I am the best at drawing sceneries.

I would like to go to college early because I love musical theater. Recently, I discovered that Faulkner University has musical theater classes that I could take. I would like to go to college at the age of twelve because when I'm done I will have more time to get the job I really want. I have never had to read or write anything I was not interested in. My parents let me read and write everything I wanted. I was inspired to do musical theater because I love to sing.

142

14

Ideas, Exercises, and Experiments

For we are God's handiwork, created in Christ Jesus to do good
works, which God prepared in advance for us to do.
—EPHESIANS 2:10

The Bible shows us the importance of loving God and teaching our children to do the same. Here are some things you can do with your children that are ways you can teach them while they are at home with you. Take advantage of the time, even if they are at school most of the day. It's a mind-set.

Ask Questions

Here's an example of a naturally occurring teachable moment in life and questions you can ask your kids:

• Count the number of fireflies you see each evening when you go for a walk.

- If your neighborhood sprays for mosquitoes, do you think this might reduce their numbers?
- Would you believe your local government if they told you it wouldn't harm you?
- Would you expect a higher incidence of disease in the area? How would a researcher go about finding this data? How might a decrease in the mosquito population affect the natural environment? Is human comfort a higher goal than the possible effect on the environment?

Every question has the potential for learning and helping your child grow. It's also a chance to have some fun and engage in some wonderful conversations.

Experiment

Take a look at your tap water. What exactly does the city put into it to keep it "safe" for us? If you buy a microscope and put a drop of it on a slide and a drop of bottled water on another slide, do you see a difference? This ninth-grade-level work can be done at age seven or eight. What happens when you get peanut butter or jelly on a slide? What happens if you look at the slides at night with a flashlight? (Okay, I'll answer this one for you . . . You're becoming a true geek or are on the road to starting college by twelve.)

If your kids are not being challenged in school or they are just bored during the summer, you can give them a little extra assignment that they might like to research:

Go to YouTube.com, then in the search bar type "cool experiments to do at home" and see what comes up. There are so many really neat things to try but as always, ask your kids which one they want to try. Remind them never to play with matches or do any experiments without your supervision. And teach your kids the acronym PUMA ("personally unsettling material") so that when they hear you say it, they know it is time to click away.

If they have no affinity for chemistry or physics, try to relate these subjects in some way to what it is they enjoy watching on YouTube or reading about on other websites. Keep refining your searches in line with the child's interests, all the while thinking about how to incorporate other subjects into their learning experience. This is the time to show how powerful tailored and accelerated learning is for any observers. Together with the child, plot out all the experiments they want to try.

Once you leap from "entertainment"-oriented fun and they begin to grasp how these things are important in society, they will be more interested in collegiate-like curriculum leading toward a degree in their favorite specialty. If the child is not controlling the mouse, *you* are having too much fun. Let them take control and as we always say, parents just need to get out of the way!

> AS WE ALWAYS SAY, PARENTS JUST NEED TO GET OUT OF THE WAY!

An Art Project

Another fun homeschooling exercise is to gather a table setting full of pots and pans, vases, candlesticks, cutlery, and assorted eye-catching ornaments. Then tell your children, no matter what their age, they can't move anything on the table but they have to choose at least one of the objects to draw. Or they can choose to draw the entire setting.

If you have the energy for it, you can supervise their painting of the drawings when they are finished. Part of what makes this enjoyable is simply finding the right objects in the house, the garden, the kitchen, or even the garage to place on the table. It is also a way of getting kids to clean up the table, with the reward being you'll play this game with them afterward.

Math Projects

Do a Google search of "math for kids" or go to the library. There are innumerable math games you can play. Don't teach them the Internet is too evil. Just teach them to use it wisely and cautiously like a hot stove.

One of Katie's favorite places to take the little kids when I ask her to entertain them is SheppardSoftware.com. This site has counting games that keep Thunder in a chair for a little while. On this site, Lorennah likes Fruit Shoot to practice her math facts. Mariannah can also practice her multiplication as she plays a game.

Our kids know how to search online to find many sites like this one where they can practice their math skills without Mom. Mom is there for the complicated questions. But if it is too complicated there is always Hannah!

Biology and Chemistry Projects

Lean on your local homeschool co-ops if you lack or can't afford the proper equipment to do science experiments. We found that our biology/premed-major child, Serennah, did not need any lab experience prior to college. All of our kids waited until college to start their labs and did very well in them. They started with the basics from the first day and went as far as they liked according to their majors.

Catching butterflies and small critters is still classic good fun. Once you do, go on the Internet and see if you can discover what they are. Use a sharp knife that you never plan to eat with again and dissect your findings. There are endless experiments you can do with chemistry sets, but start with a small, safe chemistry set and always supervise. Our oldest had one but there were always too many little ones around. Keep in mind, we never did many experiments and our students learned all their chemistry, physics, and biology lab skills entirely in college. I believe that we bought this set at a homeschool conference when we lived in California. I worry a lot about chemicals in our home.

HomeTrainingTools.com has a nice variety of sets if you really want to let your kids loose in your kitchen. Good luck!

Challenge Convention

Parents should be willing to challenge contemporary science. Just because theories become widely accepted does not mean that they are always correct.

You can have kids write a one-page Internet research paper on the theory of dark matter, for example. Why is it inconclusive? What are the other theories? How can we prove it beyond a shadow of a doubt? Or have them explore whether shadows in space actually prove the existence of unseen objects. Or ask what they think might be out there causing spiral developments. What is their relationship to water draining in a bathtub? Or ocean waterspouts, tornadoes, hurricanes, or cyclones? Which direction do they flow in the Southern Hemisphere, in places like Peru and Australia? Or have them investigate what happens when a school of fish all swim in the same direction but one fish chooses to go a different way.

A Dance Project

Yes, this is very important and this is Kip writing. I absolutely love tap dancing. It is very masculine for your sons and helpful in preventing child obesity. Ballet will teach them culture, and jazz will make them limber, athletic, and confident on the dance floor (which their future spouses might appreciate).

A History and Politics Project

In the spirit of learning, have your child research on the Internet the reasons why eleven Colorado counties want to secede to form North Colorado. Though the object of the lesson is multifaceted, you should learn about the subject along with your child. How did Colorado come to be? What was the Louisiana Purchase? Children oftentimes form their opinions and political leanings from their parents. Ask each other questions about why you think this might be important. Have your child switch roles, arguing for the secession and then against it. Take a nonpartisan position and see what your child believes in. They are very impressionable, so you want to think through how you can present ideas fairly.

If you know nothing of a subject, that is fine. The credentials of a teacher and quality of a lesson plan are not defined so much by their substance as by their outcomes. When your child is learning along with you and you explain as you go, the questions of government, environment, geography, gun bills, and the Constitution all start to make sense.

I don't worry about subject lines crossing. That is how life works. Only in an Industrial Age classroom are things always separated out and professionalized. In the Information Age, we want to mix and merge appropriately, showing kids how these ideas all fit together in critical decision making.

A Geography Project

Plot where these four species live and breed on a world map you make. Use the four-color theorem and a legend to explain what each color represents.

- Seals
- Cicada bugs
- Storks
- *Stenotritidae* bees

More Potential Project Topics

- How many days do you have to drive by a dead armadillo before you no longer notice it? Does it stink worse the longer it remains? After a time, does your nose no longer notice? So it is with unfair taxation. At first it is bothersome, then we become indifferent. Why should taxation and government spending be a high priority (provide a one-page answer)?

- Consider the Wright Brothers Effect, the idea that the famous flying brothers might not have been the first to fly but were the most celebrated for their work. Did they still make the most significant contribution to aeronautics? Is our family a similar case in the field of education and homeschooling (prepare a two-minute oral argument)?
- When having conversations at a party, is it ethical to try to network for a job? Are lobbyists in government simply searching to meet employment needs? Is their need any less important than yours may be one day in your career field? When does it become too much and should it be regulated or left to the free market? (Five-minute discussion.)

These questions are examples of things that we talk about with our kids either around the supper table or in the car. Even if a topic is over their heads, we like to keep them stimulated and on their toes. More than being able to memorize random facts, we want them to become critical thinkers and know how to ask the right questions.

. . . .

When you teach a child, try to do it in reverse. Set up the problem and see if the child can come to the right conclusion on their own. The more they are resourceful in finding answers, the better off they are, but collective learning should not be sacrificed. Rewarding team players is crucial. Those who cannot work well with others need to be called out and taught teamwork lessons first. By listening instead of talking you make a greater difference.

—KIP HARDING

From the Kids

My Homeschooling Experience
by Mariannah (age 8)
[2013]

I like homeschooling because I am not gone so much. I will write what is on my list. I do writing, reading, science, math, and piano. In the morning I have to let our dog Pebbles out of her cage. Katrinnah and I have chores and we used to switch. But now we keep it so that I do dishes and Katrinnah sweeps because I like to do dishes. I do not like to do laundry, but we all have to help so that we have clothes.

I want to know what school feels like and go for one day. But I would not want to go every day.

When I grow up I want to be a doctor. I do not know if I want to be a surgeon or a doctor that delivers babies. I do not know what they are called. I have a science book about your body parts. I finished that book. Hannah thinks I should read the MCAT book but I think I should read another kid's science book. I guess I want to be a doctor because they help people and I like cute little babies.

Sometimes I read with Lori. We both read to Thunder.

Today this funny thing happened to me. I fell and I was hurting but I was laughing, too. I was hanging on to the swing. It was scary and funny at the same time.

I want to tell kids to homeschool because it will be fun.

I thought it would be scary to get baptized but it was fun. The water was warm.

My favorite color is blue and my favorite age is 8. My favorite old age is 18. I am 8.

15

Questions and Answers with the Brainy Bunch

Do not answer a fool according to his folly, or you yourself will be just like him.

—PROVERBS 26:4

We are often asked a variety of questions about our family and getting your kids to go to college by twelve. Here are answers to a few of the most common questions.

Question: Are your kids geniuses?

Answer: Our kids are not geniuses. They are just hard workers who are reaping the benefits of being homeschooled.

Question: What curriculum do you use?

Answer: We started out with Alpha Omega workbooks, *Saxon Math* textbooks, the Bible, and books from the library. We also use KhanAcademy.org (free!) for math. This website also offers other subjects. We let the kids choose books from the library or just use old college textbooks that we have accumulated over the years.

We believe that there is no magic curriculum. The important thing about any curriculum you choose is that it is challenging and interesting. If your child becomes frustrated with a new concept, shelve it for a while and come back to it later.

Question: Should we take a loan out for college?

Answer: Our kids are so much more focused than we were at their age, not to mention the fact that they see how much a college education costs. They are getting huge scholarships and grants but they and we are still incurring some debt for their future. So, parents: don't feel guilty about this! It is better to have an education behind them than a more expensive education ahead of them. If they waited until they were older to go to college that would be the case. Tuition prices go up every year! Although college can be very, very expensive, it all depends on your children's aspirations and where they choose to attend. Once again, parents, don't feel guilty if you can't pay cash for everything. It's a reality just like a mortgage is on a house. The degree will pay for itself in time. We consider any money spent on your child's education an investment.

Question: What sort of extracurricular activities do you get your children involved with?

Answer: Back in the year 2001, our older girls played in club soccer. We invested a lot of time and money during the seasons that they traveled with their team. We poured our energy into soccer because the girls loved playing, and as always, we wanted to be completely supportive. We were hoping that all of this hard work would lead to college scholarships. Hannah ended up being the only one who played at the collegiate level. She eventually gave it up to concentrate on her studies. The math got very intense as soon as she transferred to a four-year program.

When the boys came along, they played soccer, too, but it became evident that they would not be looking to get athletic scholarships. Interestingly, Hannah at twelve and thirteen was the same size as many of the more petite players on her women's soccer team. However, it was not like that at all with our boys. Heath finally passed his father in height as a graduate student. It was too late for Heath to play sports in an undergraduate program. So we have poured our energies into areas where our kids can excel.

This might be different with the younger kids coming along. Katrinnah is pretty tall for a ten-year-old. If she wanted to try out for a collegiate sport, we would support her. She seems to be leaning toward theater arts, though. Some well-meaning friends have recommended programs at local children's theaters. We usually just thank them for the information. We do not always explain that we choose to pursue extracurriculars at the college level. We do not want to hurt their feelings but we think it is important for others to see our kids as college students.

Similarly, when we started sharing back in 2008 that Keith had an interest in music and marching band, friends sent us info for homeschool choirs and bands in the local area. We discussed these options with Keith and we came to the conclusion together that it was important for Keith to see himself playing and performing at the college level. He had not marched in a high school band before starting at Faulkner University so there was a learning curve. He ended up doing very well once he learned how to march while playing the clarinet. He ended up becoming the section leader during his junior and senior years. He also became a co–section leader in the choir. Later he was elected by his peers as vice president and then president of the choir.

Question: What is your secret to being happy, Mona Lisa?

Answer: My husband, Kip, is my greatest example of being joyful. When things are not going well, he is the one who can always look at the bright side. Even when things are *really* bad, he shows the kids and me how to be thankful for our salvation and to count our blessings. When he is down, I try to encourage him and be his "helpmeet." It is an honor to be in this position and a great source of joy for me. When I am down, I turn to him as my soul mate. We rely on our marriage, and this example also provides our children with a great model for happiness in their lives.

Question: How do you know what your child's interests are?

Answer: This is an easy answer. *Just ask them!* If your three-year-old likes dump trucks like ours does, take him to the library and read him books about dump trucks. If your ten-year-old has been praying and asking God to reveal if medicine is His calling in his life, dump a stack of college-level textbooks on his desk and see what happens. It is okay if some or most of the material is over his head. Your child will either realize that medicine is not what he thought it was, *or* your child will be challenged by the advanced material to do more research.

DO NOT UNDERESTIMATE WHAT MATERIAL YOUR CHILD CAN UNDERSTAND.

Do not underestimate what material your child can understand. Allow them to dream big and shoot for the stars.

Question: Have you ever had sibling rivalry in your house?

Answer: So far, our kids have each chosen different majors so we have not seen the expected rivalry. The closest thing might have been when Serennah graduated from Huntingdon College at seventeen and then Heath graduated from the same college at fifteen. But Serennah is such a loving and supportive big sister who loves to tell people how her little brother "broke her record." Heath, in turn, recognizes that he got a head start because he had three older sisters who taught him in addition to his parents. He learned a lot of things about life besides just math facts from these sisters.

Question: What if you have a child diagnosed with ADHD? Should you consider homeschooling them?

Answer: Although we are not learning-disability experts, we have heard of many cases where homeschooling has helped kids with ADD and ADHD. It may even help them in more ways than you can imagine. Not only will the child be freed from the distractions of all the other students and activities going on in the classroom, but they will be able to focus as long as they need to or wish to on the topic at hand and not have to jump from subject to subject at the whim of a school bell. In addition, you will both benefit from lowered levels of stress due to things like bullying because your child is different, pressure to perform on standardized tests, having to deal with unhelpful school officials, and your child being just plain bored! Many, many ADHD children are extremely intelligent, and when they're given material that meets their level of need and intensity, their ADHD symptoms tend to lessen and sometimes disappear altogether.

Question: How is your youngest developing?

Answer: Thunder is his own little character, usually in the background in one of his superhero costumes. The kid can run really fast. And he loves driving his little electric four-wheeler around the house. He has a huge personality. He will act shy for a little while when a stranger comes around, then once he trusts the person, the thunder comes out. Give him a plastic sword and a shield and he will pulverize you. His big brother Seth wrestles with him all the time and when they both turn on their dad, Thunder will try to make him tap out, but that is just not going to happen.

Question: Where do your older kids live now?

Answer: Hannah lives down the street in our rental house with a roommate. She attends church with us and currently has an account on ChristianMingle.com. She does not want to casually date because she believes in waiting for the husband that God wants to send her. She always tells those wanting to talk to her that they have to go through Dad first. That is a pretty good filter. It leaves only a handful of hopefuls. She hasn't met "the one" yet.

Rosannah lives in New York City attending Cooper Union. We encouraged her to marry at the age of nineteen. She and the love of her life, Sergio, are still settling into their new area after moving from San Francisco. They are in need of a good church in the big city to welcome them in and help keep their faith strong.

Serennah is now serving in Bethesda, Maryland. She works long hours as a resident, but she enjoys the work deeply.

Heath turns eighteen in November and we believe he will stay at home for a time. He is currently working in a small business partnership and is hoping that he will be able to make this start-up grow.

Question: What does conversation around your dinner table sound like?

Answer: We are usually not politically correct. We toss around conspiracy theories and controversial subjects to get the kids thinking about "adult" subjects. We like to debate everything. Without any disrespect to the lives that were lost on 9/11, we discuss those tragic events openly. For instance, we ask our kids, "Why did the second World Trade Center tower fall first, when it was hit second?" One theory is that it was hit lower than the first, so the water sprinkler systems would have had more water pressure, thus flooding the floors faster. This would have caused more weight on the building sooner, causing it to fall first. But it doesn't take away from the heroic efforts of the firemen. Building 7 fell and wasn't even hit by a plane. In the Pentagon, survivors reported fire on top of the water because aviation fuel is lighter than water. We tell our kids, no matter what the captain says, even when they say everything is "fine" or "Please stay in your seats," that may be the time for them to be on heightened alert and plan their next move. The dinner table conversations can also turn to positive things like the beautiful tributes in lights that are done every year at ground zero or the terrific architecture in the new buildings or the stories of the heroes who emerged that terrible day. When we tell our children, "Let's roll," when it is time to go somewhere, they have a historic context to think upon with Todd Beamer. They know our expectations for them are that they will be leaders, not followers, and always try to learn from the lessons of the past.

Another topic might be something like this: Why did the lunar lander have such large pads? Scientists believed the moon was millions of years old and at the present rate of dust accumulation, the lander should have sunk several feet in, yet it only sank a few inches.

Or here's another: If the moon has been getting one inch farther from Earth per year for millions of years, it would have been part of Earth at some point and escaped the Earth's gravity already. This topic brings up more questions when researching the age of the earth. Some people believe in the "young earth theory." Again, we are merely suggesting areas that students may want to research beyond what is in their textbooks. Sometimes we need to raise questions that make us a little uncomfortable in search of the truth.

This is what you will hear around our supper table. Sometimes, when the questions are being asked, we do not always find the answers. It is just good that our kids are learning to be critical thinkers. They are also learning to not be afraid to ask questions or challenge ideas.

Question: How do you teach your kids how to interact with adults?
Answer: The following is a good example of what we are working toward with our kids:

A couple of years ago I (Mona Lisa) had the opportunity to briefly take my eight-year-old daughter, Katrinnah, into the nursing facility where I worked to get a form signed. I knew that it was very important before we entered the facility for me to take the time to explain to her what kinds of things she would see. I told her that she might see diabetic patients who have multiple amputations, stroke victims with noticeable paralysis, mental health patients whose behavior will seem shockingly inappropriate. I also explained that she should not be afraid and not stare and always smile politely at the residents. Then I asked her to hold her questions until after we exited the facility. I did not want her to embarrass anyone by asking something too personal.

I have seen cases where some kids are raised to ask any question they would like (which is a good thing), but the child is not taught about their timing in asking such questions. For instance, when we first moved to Kansas, a child asked his mother why my skin was so dark because he had never met a very sunburned Hispanic. This innocent little boy always referred to me as "the brown lady." He had just not been exposed to people of different colors. This did not bother me at all, but some people might have been. I did learn that I should train my kids to have the social awareness of *when* it is appropriate to ask certain questions.

Going back to my story, Katrinnah did have lots of questions after we left the facility and we had a wonderful teaching time. I did not give any of this a second thought because we have been relishing these wonderful teaching moments ever since our oldest daughter asked, "Why is the moon following us?" as she looked out the car window. Even recently Hannah still will e-mail or call us asking for wisdom in dealing with professional issues or co-workers.

It wasn't until just recently, when a co-worker brought in her thirteen-year-old daughter to the same nursing facility to finish up some paperwork, that it really dawned on me that some kids are not raised to be socially aware of their surroundings. This girl was very surprised when a mentally retarded young man wheeled his chair up to her so he could stare at her. She then proceeded to say loudly, "Why is he staring at me?" She seemed very upset at the resident. Her mother then explained that he just did not know any better. I was surprised that this girl of thirteen reacted in such a way. It would have been good for her to have received a "briefing," as we like to call them, before entering the facility. We do hope, for the girl's sake, that her mother took the time on the way home to really educate her so that next time she will be more socially aware and have a more appropriate reaction.

We know it is so much easier to give a child a short answer

and then say, "Now go play. I am tired." Really taking the time to talk to your kids is probably a better use of time than just drilling math facts. They can do that with flash cards on their own time. When they are with you they can have your undivided attention. It is during these times that a parent may find out that their child is interested in pursuing a career in medicine, nursing, psychiatry, physical therapy, etc.

Question: What do you think is the future of homeschooling?

Answer: Kip and I believe that homeschooling is the best way to educate children. But we also know that there are many people out there who cannot homeschool or are afraid to homeschool. As another option, we would someday like to see TAG schools everywhere. TAG stands for "tailored, accelerated, and godly." These schools could offer a few different types of services.

There could be full-time schools where parents who cannot homeschool could drop off their kids. Other parents could enroll their homeschooled kids part-time for only the courses that they need help with, e.g. foreign languages, music, ACT/SAT preparation, or advanced math. Also, classes could be offered to parents who want training in how to homeschool their own children.

TAG schools would not accept any government funding so that subjects could be taught with religion in mind. Each child would be instructed according to their interests and ability. A child would accelerate according to their ability, not age. And early entrance into college would be encouraged because this is the smartest way to earn high school and college credits simultaneously. There would have to be a very, very low student–teacher ratio in order for the school to be truly effective.

It would be so wonderful if the school could also offer scholarships to kids from one-parent homes who are struggling in the public school system and are desperately looking for something better.

We would hope that the students at the TAG schools would be so motivated by being able to graduate early that local universities would seek out these students, even to the point of recruiting them.

We would love for this model to be duplicated all over the US and the world. The right to homeschool should never be taken away, but for those who are unable, a second option to homeschooling should be a TAG school. We can improve our education system by offering the public school system some healthy competition.

From the Kids

Lorennah's View of Homeschooling
age five (typed by Mom!)
[2013]

I like my calculator. It tells you the answers. I know 2+2=4. I like to read *Dick and Jane*. I do not want to go to school. I want to still be home-schooled because I like my mom to be my teacher.

What is the highest number? Does it just keep on going?

Mona Lisa: "Yes, it keeps going. But tell me about homeschooling."

I do copies of work sheets. Well, I like to do "Tumblebooks."

I do not know what else to say.

16

A Beautiful Dream

"A new command I give you: Love one another. As I have loved you, so you must love one another. By this everyone will know that you are my disciples, if you love one another."

—JOHN 13: 34-35

Before Serennah started at AUM, another university was reviewing Serennah's transcript and the Dean of Admissions seemed open to our situation. I got the feeling that Serennah was going to be allowed to take one class at that university. It was a Spanish class that Rosannah, our second oldest daughter, was going to start soon. We thought that this would be the perfect opportunity for her to get her feet wet in college for the first time.

Things changed, however, as soon as the Dean spoke to the university's attorney. He soon became opposed to the idea. The Dean stated that the school is geared toward working adults who are pursuing their degrees through evening, weekend, and lunch-hour classes. The point is that even though their primary students are adults, we suspected that age was the primary factor for the opposition. What a shame!

We just took our business elsewhere and figured it was their loss.

This brings up something very valuable we are educating into our children. Most schools are teaching tolerance. We are teaching our kids to not just tolerate others but to embrace every race.

Kip and I went to Independence High School in the 80s. It was a good time to be there. The school district had a program where kids were bussed in from all over San Jose to participate in the school Fine Arts program to promote diversity. I came from the Hispanic side of town and got to take drama and dance classes. There were a few great football players in my drama class who came to our school to play on our large football team. The result for Kip and I was that we had students of all races in our social circles. There were plenty of people dating outside of their race. In a sense, we were color blind.

It was not until we moved to Kansas and then Alabama that I learned that people viewed us as a biracial couple. We learned quickly that down here in the South, some people simply tolerate one another like one tolerates a pebble in their shoe. We want something better for our kids. We want our kids to look into the hearts of the people that they meet, not just the color of their skin. We have heard people say, "I am not a racist. I have a friend who is _____." They proceed to give a list of all of their "friends" and their races. We believe the true test is how would these people feel if their child brought home a new boyfriend or girlfriend of another race. This is the acid test.

We believe that biracial children can grow up embracing both sides of their family tree. We tell our kids that if everyone in America inter-married, there would be less tension and no need for surveys asking us to report what race we consider ourselves. Kip is white and had a grandfather from Spain. Kip's middle name is Lopez. It bothers him when government forms force him to check the "White, not of Hispanic origin" box.

Back in 2003 when we were looking for a house to buy, we asked the realtor to show us homes in a diverse neighborhood because we had heard that Montgomery suffers from de facto segregation. We wanted no part in that. We wanted our kids to have the same type of culturally enriched upbringing that we had enjoyed in Silicon Valley. The realtor did a good job with the first house, but she kept hinting that we might want to try "other" neighborhoods. She meant white neighborhoods. We did humor her and looked at the other properties but decided to buy the first home in the nicely mixed area. Unfortunately, many of the military members stationed here are led by realtors to the east side or outside of town. So, Montgomery is suffering from "white flight" just like our native San Jose has.

After another assignment, we returned to Montgomery in 2007, and learned that not much had changed. Sadly, prejudice is alive and well down here in the South. This time Kip was the one who suffered. He wanted a haircut because he had an interview for the doctoral program at historically black college/university (HBCU) Alabama State. He visited several barbershops near the university and was turned away. Sure, they had excuses that they were too busy. But Kip quickly got the implied message, "We do not cut white people's hair." It was devastating and unbelievable! We seriously thought about trying again with a hidden camera.

More recently, I had an African-American coworker tease me about being Osama Bin Ladin's cousin while the rest of the African-American staff laughed. I certainly would be proud to be from the Middle East. But it is wrong for people to laugh at someone because of his/her race. Needless to say, she and I paid a visit to the Human Resources Department and the teasing stopped. Also, there were a couple of African-American nurses there who were given a hard time about choosing to date outside of their race.

Despite all of its problems, we love living in Montgomery, the birthplace of the civil rights movement. Our kids have visited Dr. King's church and home. They know that he was a Godly man who truly loved all people and had a beautiful dream.

People everywhere need to stop trying to get back at others for the sins of their fathers. We have decided to teach our kids to do more than just "tolerate" others but to embrace every race.

17

Everybody Has Tough Times

For his anger lasts only a moment, but his favor lasts a lifetime;
weeping may stay for the night, but rejoicing comes in the morning.
—PSALM 30:5

I (Mona Lisa) can still remember one of the scariest moments of my life. It was in 2001 when Seth was only five months old and being operated on. He was having kidney surgery and was under anesthesia for several hours. I waited and prayed and hoped, and then prayed some more, yet each passing moment felt like an eternity. I was so afraid that he was too little for surgery and that he would die on the operating table.

With each second, my heart broke a little more. Of course it all turned out all right in the end, but it was still a very tough time for us. Another challenging moment as a parent was in 2006 when Rosannah met and fell in love with Sergio while studying abroad in Mexico. I thought that she was too young, but Kip (the romantic that he is) encouraged her to find out if he really was "the one." He was all for her marrying young. He reminded me that we were seventeen when we fell in love. Of course there is a double standard when it is happening to your own daughter. He trusted in her judgment and over time encouraged her to marry as soon as Sergio had gained Kip's approval. Once again, Kip really knows how to trust what is in the hearts of our children, whether they're choosing a career or a spouse.

All parents have moments like these, and Kip and I have had our share. Most parents know what it is like to be up all night with a sick child. The night can feel extra long. We have learned over the last twenty-seven years of marriage and ten kids later that if you just hang on to God's hand through the nighttime, then "this too shall pass" and "joy comes in the morning."

Sick children are one thing, but most marital problems stem from financial difficulties. Sadly, many couples argue about money. If we had money, we would probably argue about which vacation we should go on. In our case, the arguments result from the stress that comes from being short at the end of the month. Some would think that having the mom go out of the home to earn more money would solve all of the problems, but we have found that this can cause even more tension. I feel guilty if I am not working and we are struggling to pay bills. However, if I am at work I still feel guilty because I know that my family is not getting my best.

When we were newlyweds, Kip and I resembled the country song "Livin' on Love." Our first place together was in a little trailer park in Enterprise, Alabama, right outside of Fort Rucker. Kip was there for his army helicopter mechanic school. It was a very sweet and tender time for both of us. Then we moved to Manhattan, Kansas, and all was well for a time but life did get hard episodically.

It was during this period that we had to learn how to really communicate. I had to learn how to follow Kip's lead. We moved again to a little town called McFarland, Kansas. Kip always reminds me of the legendary advice my stepdad gave him when it comes to marriage—"no refunds!" This is a pragmatic way of saying, "She is yours now, so the two of you must work it out whenever you have difficulties." Kip has passed on the same advice to Sergio to assure him we never want to meddle, but we are counting on the two of them to make it through the tough times.

KIP ALWAYS REMINDS ME OF THE LEGENDARY ADVICE MY STEPDAD GAVE HIM WHEN IT COMES TO MARRIAGE— "NO REFUNDS!"

It was a blessing of sorts to be away from family in the sense that I could not "run home to Mama" every time we had an argument. We had no one else to run and complain to, so we had to both give in and resolve to work things out. Young children need to hear family stories like these to build a sense of understanding about true love. It endures through hardships and the sacrifices are well worth it.

Kip finished his first three-year tour in the army at Fort Riley, Kansas, a couple of months after our second child was born. He was taking classes at night at Topeka Technical College and working during the day. I cannot even remember what the job was because there were several, both temporary and part-time. He did what he could whenever he could to put food on the table. I really fell in love with him all over again during this time period because he was such a good provider and father to our girls. Our girls came along so quickly that Kip referred to their births as "Bing, bang, boom."

Despite our financial hardship, Kip knew in his heart that God would take care of us. He wanted lots of kids and was trusting in the Lord to provide. Kip was doing his part by being a man and getting up every morning and going to whatever thankless job he had at the time. And he was determined to get an education. Kip did not end up using the technical degree that he earned but this degree did help him get accepted into flight school in the upcoming years. I, on the other hand, was weaker in my faith and wanted to put off having more kids. I was working the night shift as a certified nurse aide when I got pregnant with Serennah. I applied for a medical card to cover the pregnancy. I was very happy to have another precious baby but worried about the future. Kip was confident that God would help us finish school and continue to provide. His faith had him convinced that somehow I would manage working and having a third baby.

When I found out that I had been accepted into the LPN program, my first reaction was, "I cannot do this." Kip's reaction was, "God will work it all out." And God did. He always does. Serennah's birth was perfectly timed by her Creator, even though we had to take her to the babysitter when she was less than two weeks old in order for me to finish my nursing program. My heart was broken to have to do this but we were in survival mode.

After nursing school, Kip started his warrant officer flight training back at Fort Rucker and I only had to work a couple of days a week. Although I enjoyed these preschool years, I started to think that three kids might be enough for me. I had my hands full. After graduating flight school, at the top of his class (distinguished graduate), Kip had come a long way from being an uninterested C student at our public high school. He decided to finish his associate's degree at Kansas State University at the Salina campus. This is where we actually bought some workbooks for Hannah and started some formal lessons. Kip entertained her with his calculus homework in the evenings while I worked the three-to-eleven shift at the nursing home next to our apartment. This was when something clicked with Hannah and math.

When Kip earned his AS degree, he went back to working here and there. There just was not much opportunity in the rural area of Kansas where we were living. This was the time where I could not give up my insecurities and just homeschool. I chose at the last minute to put Hannah in a private school, do private day care in our home, and work in nursing on the weekends. We lived paycheck to paycheck. Times were hard but I can honestly say that we always knew that things would get better. I longed for the day that I would not have to work and I could finally homeschool.

During the years when our older girls were in private school, I felt guilty that I was not homeschooling. It was our tough financial situation that was getting in the way. The winters in Kansas were hard on us Californians and we never could get used to the tornado sirens sending us to our basement. We loved our church and friends but we were so ready for a new adventure!

The military life was good and it was fun meeting new friends at each assignment. Kip and I had to deal with the stresses of moving around but our kids were sheltered from this because all of their "classmates" moved with them. And they always knew who their teacher was going to be at each new place—me! This is one reason we believe that homeschooling fits in perfectly with the military lifestyle. And no one will blame you for trying to homeschool if you are forced to move frequently. We know from consulting that even the most resistant in-laws are willing to go along with it if it makes things easier for the little "nomads."

Early on Kip figured out that we should not be afraid to fail. As a family, we would ask around the dinner table, "What is the worst thing that could happen?" Whenever we ask this question out loud and everyone agrees that the worst thing would not be the end of the world, we pray again and then usually decide to go for it. This process of praying and going for it has become a way of life for us.

We are raising our kids to put up their spiritual antennas so they can hear God's voice and then not be afraid to act. In the Bible, God asks people to step out of their comfort zones and trust Him. We need to not be afraid to try new things. Sometimes things just don't work out and God closes a door. That is okay. We just move on and try something else until we get it right. We are raising our kids to not be afraid of failure.

With each new child applying to college, I would get nervous. I would begin to doubt and ask, "Is *this* child ready?" I would have to be careful not to share all of my insecurities with the child. Kip is our kids' biggest fan. The kids are so pumped up after one of Daddy's pep talks. They know that they have every right to be in a college classroom. I am not sure why I get nervous because they always exceed my expectations. I guess moms tend to see their kids as young and helpless. I get over it as soon as I see the excitement in their eyes after the first class session goes really well. So far, so good. Thank God. No one has dropped dead during an exam.

In 2013, we have the nice challenge of figuring out what Keith will do with his music degree at the age of fifteen. He would like to go to graduate school. We are looking in our local area but are having some trouble. We are exploring the possibility of his starting his own business. He wants to compose music for films. We hope that he won't have to move away so young. This time around we have the luxury of having kids living in other states. Keith is looking in the DC area, where Serennah lives, and New York, where Rosannah is. Honestly, we want Keith at home with us as long as possible, but if the Lord opened some doors and he could live with his sisters, we might consider it. I say "might" because He would have to make it very clear and give us peace about it.

As we are preparing our seventh child (Katrinnah) to enter college, we feel pretty comfortable with how to help our kids make the transition from being homeschoolers to being part-time college students and then, eventually, full-time and on their own (academically). The tough challenges seem to always be related to finances. Once again our financial issue got in the way this past summer when Keith and Seth were unable to take classes. Part of our accelerated success has been that we believe in schooling all year-round, even at the college level. So now Keith will be taking a whole lot of credits in his last two semesters just to graduate on time. We sure do not like doing things this way but he is a trouper and has always been willing to work hard.

Keith was able to work independently when he was finishing up high school. I had to work the three-to-eleven shift during his last year of high school. He did very well but did earn a couple of B's because I was not always around to make sure he was being taught the material to the point of learning 100 percent. Where most homeschoolers are able to get all A's, Keith had to settle for a couple of B's, but it was not his fault. Sadly, once again, the bad economy forced his mom out of the home and he did the best he could. He is on the dean's list now semester after semester, so we are thankful that he was not "permanently damaged." It is too bad that tough financial times can have this type of effect. The blessing is that in college there are tutor centers where students can get all of the help that they need. My kids have made good use of these centers and we are so thankful for that.

When we consult with others, we try to stress the importance of "teaching yourself out of a job." What we mean by this is your child will outdo you and you'll have to send them to college to keep them learning. As parents, you want to be there to answer 100 percent of their questions so that they are learning 100 percent of the material that they have chosen and they can earn all A's. Why would you not do this? This is a wonderful benefit of homeschooling. If you do this under ideal circumstances, your child is getting a grade-A education. However, if hard times come (e.g. illness, unemployment, military deployment, the birth of a new baby, having to move, or taking care of an aging parent), then you have a student who can now at least earn B's on their own.

Another challenge in our family has been a logistical one. I am sure that families everywhere deal with the same issue. Our younger kids, fortunately, still get to sleep in later than the college and working kids get to do. There is usually someone at home old enough to watch them so that I do not have to haul the little ones around everywhere as we get the bigger kids in college to class on time. It is usually in the afternoon that we have to all ride to pick up kids from college. The younger ones usually have their backpacks ready to go in the car so that they can catch up on reading or writing in their journals while we commute. The load gets a little lighter each time someone gets to be babysitting age or driving age. The more kids there are, the trickier the logistics get. But with that comes the additional helpers.

Kip likes to have the kids post a color-coded Microsoft Excel spreadsheet on the inside of the front door with the children's combined schedules in time slots so he can help manage what has to get done each day and who has to be where at what time. He loves spreadsheets and he says by having the kids work together to create it, everyone gets a good idea of what is going on. Color-coded scheduling really works well for parents who are just trying to survive and gives new meaning to the emphasis we place on not leaving any child behind.

> COLOR-CODED SCHEDULING REALLY WORKS WELL FOR PARENTS WHO ARE JUST TRYING TO SURVIVE.

I keep telling myself that it will all balance out and eventually get easier. This hope gets me through the crazy days.

As I was writing these words today, I had so many interruptions and errands to run that just meeting our deadline for this book has been a challenge. In 2007, we started writing in a journal during our "free time" and it was more like a hobby. When we posted it online and we saw that there really was an interest in our story, we went back and wrote more in order to bring everyone up-to-date. Then after a *Today* show segment on our family aired, we signed a book deal with Simon & Schuster. Now our dream of having a *real* book has come true. I just wanted to sit and write today but I had to be up at five A.M. to send Kip off for his one-hour commute to work, consult over the phone with a single mom who is having difficulty homeschooling her son, drive Keith to his first day of class, hand him my PayPal card (thank God the payment posted for that phone consultation) so he could buy his textbook for class today, then figure out how to juggle money.

"If You Have Never Had Your Debit Card Denied While Trying to Make a Purchase, You Have Not Lived!"

One day while I was apologizing to Serennah for not having the money to pay for something that she needed, she pointed out that our lack of finances has kept us humble. We do not have any high-maintenance spoiled brats in this household. We have never missed a meal; some of those blessed meals have consisted of beans and rice (nutritionally okay but harder for Kip to swallow), but we were still thankful. I told our kids that if you have never had your debit card denied while trying to make a purchase, you have not lived! I was joking at the time, but as I thought about it some more, I agreed with Serennah. These humbling moments keep us from getting too proud.

. . . .

An eternal question about children is, how should we educate them? Politicians and educators consider more school days in a year, more science and math, the use of computers and other technology in the classroom, more exams and tests, more certification for teachers, and less money for art. All of these responses come from the place where we want to make the child into the best adult possible, not in the ancient Greek sense of virtuous and wise, but in the sense of one who is an efficient part of the machinery of society. But on all these counts, the soul is neglected.

—THOMAS MOORE

Thunder's World by Mona Lisa Harding
Age 3
[2013]

I asked Thunder if he likes homeschooling and he said, "No, I want to stay with you." Obviously, he did not understand my question. He then proceeded to jump into my lap and ask to nurse. Yes, he is three and a half and still nurses—not for nutrition, just for comfort. He needs comforting when he is sleepy, if he falls and skins his knee, or if he gets into trouble and wants to make amends. After seeing the cover of *Time* magazine with the mother nursing her preschooler, I started to ask Thunder to wait until he was at home to nurse. I understand that people get a little weird when they see an older child nursing. Americans just don't get it. Attachment parenting does not make kids "too attached." We believe that it is part of "the greenhouse effect": keep them close while they are young, and they will grow up feeling secure. We do not stress over when it is time to wean a child or move them out of our room. Just like the way we educate our kids, we allow the child to let us know when they are ready to be more independent.

Since Thunder is pretty much with me *all* the time, I get the privilege of answering *all* of his questions. He, like all children, is naturally curious. So I get to correct the funny little sentences that he puts together and explain why this is and why that is. Why, why, why? I just love it. Even if he does not yet understand all of the answers I give him, I can see the little wheels in his head turning. It is so precious. The big kids love it, too. Just recently, as Thunder sat in his booster seat at the table eating Cheerios with honey and wearing his Winnie the Pooh costume, he asked his siblings, "Is Pooh Bear is a Christian?" I overheard the giggling at his choice of words and then Heath shared that Pooh Bear was probably Anglican and part of the Church of England. Seth philosophized that indeed Pooh Bear must be because he is just a bear, after all, and therefore created by God for His glory, and "all dogs go to heaven," right? Katrinnah mentioned that Rabbit was a complete heathen because he is so mean. Another child mentioned that Piglet was very gentle and sweet and that the "meek will inherit the Earth." Then the kids tried to diagnose Tigger's delusions of grandeur and they concluded that he probably needed some kind of therapy.

Anyway, the point is that my kids are the loveliest bunch of kids who enjoy each other's company and love that they have nine siblings. As child number ten, Thunder is very secure at home and may grow up wanting to take some risks in life, e.g. skydiving or flying with the Thunderbirds. At home Thunder gets to soak it all in and grow up in a house full of people who are willing to take the time to help him learn.

18

Teaching Can Be Exciting

We have different gifts, according to the grace given to each of us.
If your gift is prophesying, then prophesy in accordance with your
faith; if it is serving, then serve; if it is teaching, then teach.
—ROMANS 12:6–7

There are a lot of terms and theories educators use when it comes to how to make the art of teaching more of a scientific adventure. A short search of Wikipedia reveals a lot. Wikipedia, by the way, is to some graduate professors a nightmare website because anyone can post to it, even without credentials. What is the world coming to anyway?! We think of it as free thought. In any event—and this list is by no means all-inclusive—one may find terms like "classical conditioning," "operant conditioning," "transformative learning," "constructivism," "multiple intelligences," "multimedia learning," "learning style theory," "instructional theory," "connectivism," "cognitive restructuring," etc. The intellectual thoughts on learning quickly become overwhelming and a parent or teacher can get lost in all the different ideas on how the brain works.

I like to boil it down to what matters to the average person wanting to learn. If it interests the student, they will keep coming back. So keep it interesting by their definition—not yours. If a boy likes video games, tie in the game to his learning experience. Don't have him count how many bad guys he can kill in five minutes' time. That is actually dangerous! Keep things constructive. "How many rescues can you make?" "How many jumps does it take to finish this level?" "Why would knowing statistics help you as a gamer?" "How might you approach the game differently?" "What is your high score?" "What is your mean score?" "What is your median score?" "What is your mode score?" "How can we apply the idea of 'leveling up' to real life?" You have to start somewhere as a parent or educator, right?

All these terms you will forget over time, but looking them up with your child on the Internet can be fun. Along the way, you'll see what things interest your child. You'll also learn to stay on track together. If you both follow a rabbit trail, that is actually a good thing so long as you also stick to meeting the goals you set out to meet. Create some simple objectives and then have fun as you learn. Keeping your eyes focused on what is important is a tough learning skill.

The Internet wants to reveal all of Victoria's Secrets to your child. Teach them the real secret to success in life is to overcome temptation. A wonderful example of this can be seen when Jim Bob and Michelle Duggar's kids call out "Nike." What they are essentially saying is that a less-than-modest woman is walking by and we would all do best just to look down at our shoes until she passes by. Their humility is a clear sign of intelligence and is something that will help all of them go far. Our family has a similar system when using the Internet. I like to use the acronym "PUMA," which

> THE INTERNET WANTS TO REVEAL ALL OF VICTORIA'S SECRETS TO YOUR CHILD.

stands for "personally unsettling material." If I say "PUMA" while one of the kids is searching the Internet, it is time to click onto something else. Pumas look cool on your feet, not on your Internet device. You can place Post-it notes on your children's computers and on their mirrors reminding them in an acronym you borrow or create yourself, like "WWJD," when it comes to what to wear, what website to view or not view, etc. Remember, helping to build character into your child is your first parental duty and is one that cannot be delegated to the state or their peers.

If you really want your kids to read and they would much rather climb a tree, simply compromise. "Okay, sweetie, you can climb the tree but only if you read your book while you are up there. But don't go too high!" "You want to go ice-skating at the mall? Okay, honey, but first I want you to teach me a few things. Please Google-search safe techniques for proper ice-skating or how many injuries are caused each year in winter sports, or the physics involved in making ice-skaters spin faster when they bring their head and arms in. You can explain it all to me and show me when we are on the ice."

The best part about teaching young children is that most everything for them is new. Because it is new, it can be exciting. They have bright, loving eyes. My kids will do just about any chore for an ice cream or fulfill any study request for a trip to the movies. Are my kids all that much different from yours? I don't think so. "Hey, kids, how do they make ice cream anyway? Who wants to Internet-search it?" On the drive to the store, I might ask, "How much money does a Hollywood actor make? Who can give me the answer the fastest?" "How hard did Danny DeVito work to get accepted at an audition to finally prove he is a great actor?" "Given the supply-and-demand principle we all live with, how hard do you think you have to work to make a good living?" We have to explain to children that talent and connections help, but ultimately it is persistence and prayer that win the day.

Why are homeschoolers consistently making such a significant positive difference to companies like Chick-fil-A? Homeschoolers recently caught the attention of the Society for Human Resource Management, which publishes *HR Magazine*. They report that employers who have hired homeschoolers are generally enthusiastic about them. Chick-fil-A, a nationwide fast-food chain, is so happy with its homeschool hires that it actively recruits them. According to Andy Lorenzen, who helps recruit Chick-fil-A's thirty thousand front-line workers, homeschoolers are a unique source of talent. "They're smart, ambitious, and very driven," Lorenzen reports. "They are loyal, diligent, and have a good work ethic."

Homeschoolers are improving their bottom line in amazing ways. That person on the other side of the counter who is a homeschool graduate might also be a premed student or doing any number of impressive things outside of work thanks to their homeschool education and positive ambition. Wall Street would do well to track which companies are actively recruiting homeschool graduates.

The homeschool phenomenon is a tsunami that is overtaking the land and we are surfing the top of it.

From the Kids

The Kind of Doctor I Want to Be
By Serennah Harding as a med student
[2012]

I will be the kind of doctor who sits with her patients beyond office or call hours to discuss their needs. I will be the kind of doctor who gives her patients her time and skills for no charge when necessary. The kind of doctor who works diligently to fulfill every promise made by her words. I will be the doctor with integrity—I will be the same person everywhere and would do everything I do with anybody watching. I will be the kind of doctor who gives the patients and family every seat in the room and takes the garbage can as her seat. I will be the doctor who takes young students under her wing to teach them everything and more than she knows. I will be the kind of doctor who jumps on a plane to a foreign country to visit one of her patients who cannot be transported. I will be the doctor who gives her time to family before patients—and to God before family. I will be the doctor who does not hold back the tears in her eyes when her patient cries over pain—and over joy.

19

What Led Us to Write Our Book

"The King will reply, 'Truly I tell you, whatever you did for one of the least of these brothers and sisters of mine, you did for me.'"
—MATTHEW 25:40

A s we near the end of our book, we want to bring to light a little on the media exposure that led to a literary agent contacting us about taking our story to the next level in book form.

When Serennah graduated in 2008 at seventeen, she got a little bit of press. Then Heath came along in 2011 and graduated at fifteen and hardly got any press because the university focused their press release around some other graduates who were affected by some terrible tornado damage in our state.

After doing some research and discovering that Serennah was probably going to be one of the youngest female doctors in the U.S. upon her graduation from medical school in 2013 at the age of twenty-two, I (Mona Lisa) sent out her photo with a short bio to some magazines and media outlets. We also discovered that Rosannah was the youngest member of the American Institute of Architects (AIA).

Finally, in the spring of 2013, we got a call from a producer at NBC's *Today* show. They were interested in our story. After a lengthy phone interview, he told us that he would call us back in a few weeks if Mr. Bob Dotson decided to include us in one of his "American Story" segments. I had just been hired for a nursing job when they called back to notify us that they would be coming out the following week to film the segment. I immediately agreed and called my new boss to ask her if she could postpone my start date a week because we were about to host a film crew.

It was such a fun three days. Our family learned a lot about how filming for television is done. It was fun for the boys to have the camera crew come out to their college campus for a day. Some friends from our homeschool group even got to be in a scene with our kids playing in our backyard with all of Seth's medieval props.

After the cameras left, it was back to the grind. I started yet another nursing job and struggled with balancing homeschooling and working. Fortunately, this time Hannah was around to help with teaching because she was only working part-time. Some days we felt like we were tag-team wrestlers. She would tag my hand when I came in the door from work as she was going out the door to work. Like always, we just had to find a way to get things done. It was probably a blessing that Keith and Seth did not have enough financial aid to attend summer school during this time because Hannah needed their help with the younger ones while I was at work.

The *Today* show finally aired in April 2013 and the e-mails started to pour in. We got many requests for radio, magazine, and podcast interviews. We were contacted by several reality TV agents, American book agents, a Chinese book agent, and a software developer who is now working on our Kickstarter project. We were invited to speak at several homeschooling conferences here in America and in Greece.

The phone rang, too. Producers from Rachael Ray's show, Queen Latifah's show, *60 Minutes* in Australia, *Fox and Friends*, *People* magazine, and the *National Enquirer* all wanted more details. We were on cloud nine. We wanted to share our story with everyone who contacted us. We had to come up with a standard e-mail that directed people to our website and an online journal for all of the details that they were looking for. There was just no other way that we could answer all of their very important questions. Many people were looking to help their kids. We wanted so much to answer each and every one personally, but it was just Kip and me. We were both working and I was taking two online college classes. Kip was also still working on his dissertation for Alabama State University. (In my opinion, ASU should count this work as a replacement to the required dissertation for his EdD, as this will touch more lives than his dissertation ever will.)

We spent many days responding to e-mails and answering the phone. After many weeks, we had sold enough copies of our online journal that we decided I could reduce my work hours. I was now spending a lot of time on the phone consulting with folks needing help with educating their kids. I eventually was able to come home from my job and it was just in time to travel to move Serennah out of her Birmingham apartment, where she was doing her rotations for med school. We stuck all of her stuff in our garage and then headed to Atlanta for her graduation.

We had a great celebration with family and friends. There were newspaper reporters and photographers there. Serennah pinned on her new rank of lieutenant (0-3) in the navy. We drove back to Montgomery for a couple of television and newspaper interviews.

Heath received a lovely standing ovation for earning a master's degree at Troy University at the age of seventeen. As a mother, it was so wonderful to hear my kids thanking God for His help and for the wonderful privilege of being homeschooled. The next day we all did laundry, got the oil changed in Serennah's car, and packed up to head to New York.

Fox and Friends was great. We got to see Michael Bolton sing onstage and Kip actually saw Geraldo Rivera in a hallway. After the interview, I checked our e-mail on Kip's iPhone and I could see the orders coming in. There were book orders and requests for consultations and general information. The phone started ringing again. I had to put it on vibrate while we literally went across the street to meet with our new editor and all of the folks at Simon & Schuster who would be helping with our book. They treated us to the best New York pizza and made us feel really special. After lunch, I checked the iPhone again and was thrilled to find that we'd experienced viral sales. By the time we went to Central Park, someone walking in the park said they had just seen us on Fox that morning. It was like being a rock star with a whole fifteen minutes of fame. So it was fun for a time.

Rachael Ray's producer never called back. *60 Minutes* of Australia lost interest. Some things worked out and some things did not. But that's the way life goes and we just really enjoyed the moment. God has a way of showing His kindness in His timing. Our children were so happy. I even got a courtesy photograph from the state of New York a few weeks later showing I had driven my van through a red light. So our children got another homeschool lesson on the problems of peer pressure and keeping up with the car in front of you in a caravan. The challenges of getting to New York were far superseded by the good times that we had once there.

20

A Mother's Encouragement

*Children are a heritage from the Lord, offspring a reward
from Him. Like arrows in the hands of a warrior are children
born in one's youth. Blessed is the man whose quiver is full of them.
They will not be put to shame when they contend
with their opponents in court.*

—PSALM 127:3–5

S on, comb your hair. Tuck in your shirt and put on a belt."
These are the words I (Mona Lisa) woke up to early this
Saturday morning as I overheard Kip giving Seth instructions as he prepared for his community service project. This Saturday morning's project was part of Huntingdon College's "Big Red Weekend"/new student orientation. Although Seth has three college semesters under his belt, he acts no differently from any other twelve-year-old boy.

We are frequently asked how our children are able to adapt to college life at such a young age. Surprisingly, it is not so much the academics that we have issues with. Our issues are with helping our kids mature. They must learn how to dress appropriately—not too casual in trendy torn jeans, yet not too nerdy, either. We want them to look stylish, modest, and nice enough that they will be taken seriously by their professors and advisers. We work hard at teaching our kids to keep up with their own laundry and hang up their clothes right out of the dryer so that they can avoid the extra chore of having to iron. Keeping a bedroom semiclean helps keep the kids organized so that they are not searching for their iPad, ID card, calculator, or driver's permit. There are days when the newest driver misses out on getting to drive to school because of a forgotten learner's permit or I have to give up my debit card so that they can buy lunch because of a forgotten wallet/purse. These challenges would be the same if they were attending a junior high or high school.

A "college by twelve" student is earning credit for all of their efforts. Our hope is that they will not have to be reminded to comb their hair and brush their teeth by the time they are driving independently and are on their own.

We have all heard of those "genius" kids who graduate college really early, at like ten or eleven. The stories are interesting. Many times the child has foreign parents, or is an only child, or has parents who are college professors. Then we quickly dismiss the story, not ever thinking that our kids could actually do this. Sure, they may be bright students, maybe even have 4.0 GPAs, but we could not see them graduating from college *this* early.

Well, this is practical advice for how the average child can start college by the age of twelve, or even eleven. Everyone in our family is of average intelligence with average IQs and average SAT/ACT scores—there are no geniuses in this bunch, just hard workers. Here is our "secret" checklist:

- If able, homeschool—not even the most prestigious private schools can give you results like this.
- Start teaching your kids to read at age four or five.
- Encourage them to read lots and lots of fun and interesting material—nothing boring.
- Talk to them often about what they want to read more about and provide additional books on those subjects (create your own themes if you like).
- Do basic math every day and skip ahead as fast as they can go. Get to prealgebra and algebra by age eight or nine. They can memorize their math facts as they are learning new concepts (e.g., do not hold them back if they get stuck on 7 x 8).
- Make them write every day, explaining spelling and grammar rules and discussing the definitions of unknown words as you edit their writing. Then they can rewrite their work, making all the necessary corrections. At first they can copy out of their favorite books (the book of Proverbs is great for character building). Then they can gradually go from a single paragraph to the five-paragraph essay.
- By age eight or nine they can be reading high school–level books in a great variety of subjects (*not* boring high school textbooks like most of us were forced to read). Give them *real* quality books. Supplementing with educational videos and TV shows always provides great family bonding time.
- Keep track of all their work and activities that are high school level so that you can put it on their transcript.

- Discuss what local college they want to attend and what kinds of courses they will want to enroll in when they get there. Do this with eight-to-ten-year-olds so that their high school courses will support what they want to major in and their personal expectations and goals are aligned with college—e.g., read anatomy books if they want to go premed or Shakespeare if they want to major in English.

- Introduce the SAT/ACT study guides by age eight or nine and sign them up to take their first exam some time after their tenth birthday. Help them set a goal to get a score above their university's entrance requirement minimum (you can elect to not have the score reported so there is no pressure). You know your child best, so keep in mind we cannot guarantee success because each child is different. Plan ahead, because there may be a limit to the number of times they can take the test. If the score is above the minimum, you can later have it sent to the university.

- Dangle the "college carrot" by letting your kids know that as soon as they finish their high school courses and get above that required SAT/ACT score, they can start taking their first college class.

- Do not let naysayers tell you that it can't be done. Just tell them about all those Harding kids who are doing it. Let God limit your child, not you. Your kids will amaze you with what they can accomplish if they are motivated and inspired. This is *your* job: to encourage and provide experiences that will inspire them.

Moms everywhere are worried about what their kids might be missing, especially homeschooling moms. This is serious business and we do not want to mess up our kids. I have always taken this job seriously. Yet, there were times where I had to rely on God's grace and just follow my heart. There were times when I felt overwhelmed with babies coming every two and a half years and moving in the military every three. There were times where I had to ask the older home-schoolers to work on their own using solution manuals or just plain figure things out on their own so I could spend time with the little ones or collapse in bed. Without my knowing it, God was providing my kids with exactly what they needed. I did feel guilty at the time, but I was just trying to survive.

What a blessing it was when just recently, we were having dinner with Serennah and Rosannah and I asked them for their honest critique of the home education they received. Both of my daughters basically said that they learned how to learn. They learned how to find their own answers. They learned how to research. They learned that if they got the wrong answer, it was okay, and to keep searching for the right one. They learned what it was like to make mistakes and then fix them.

So my answer to the mother who asks me about the holes in her children's education is just do your best to teach your kids to be independent learners and they will be able to fill in those holes on their own. You can rely on God's grace for the rest.

21

Final Words from a Proud Father

It is enough for a man to be granted a loving wife. To say we are blessed by our "brainy bunch" is putting it mildly.

Hannah, I miss our basketball games together when you were just a young girl at Vandenberg AFB and I would have to chase after you for winning. The smile on your face was almost as priceless as your mama's.

Rosannah, you got some of your back jack from your daddy. You might have a husband now but I'm still watching you, girl. Don't make me have to come to New York City to give you a whoopin'.

Serennah, just so your fellow officers can have a laugh while you are on sea duty, your childhood nicknames were Nina and Scream Bean. There's no cure for a sick parent!

Heath, how about we make a pledge to go fishing together? No Alaska fish this time.

Keith, when you play music for me I think the angels mistakenly blessed the wrong dad. Your composition and sincerity are heavenly.

Seth, you are the king's champion. No poor soul should ever have to face your military in battle.

Katrinnah, you are part of the mercy of God, who gave me a second set of daughters in no measure less than the first. King Lear could not have asked for as much.

Mariannah, you're the Cinderella of our home. Your generosity does not go unnoticed. You are a bright light in a dark world.

Lorennah, what a precious young lady you are. You can ride on my feet whenever we dance!

Thunder, it helps to have a flashing smile, have dazzling eyes, and be an explosive force for good, but enough about me . . . Just kidding. Show the world you are all that and more.

Mona Lisa, all I know is, I'm kissing this girl back in high school and the next thing I know I'm married and I've got ten kids and a love for the Latin beat. You are my heartsong!

Appendix A: Resources
All lists in no particular order.

Be shepherds of God's flock that is under your care, watching over them—not because you must, but because you are willing, as God wants you to be; not pursuing dishonest gain, but eager to serve; not lording it over those entrusted to you, but being examples to the flock.
—I PETER 5:2–3

Since we're homeschoolers, we are used to changing the rules. There's never one single way to do something. Choosing the resources that we use is a good example of that. We've learned by trial and error. Our hope is that some of these valuable tools we've used in homeschooling will help you, too.

Best Places to Buy Supplies

The best place for supplies is the library because it is free (as long as you are not late in returning them). This allows your child(ren) to figure out what their interests are without a big investment.

- ChristianBook.com will mail you a nice thick paper catalog that your kid(s) can browse through and help you decide what you should buy.

- AOP.com is where to find Alpha Omega workbooks in almost any subject for every grade level. This is a great way to know what grade-level work your child can do.
- HSLDA.org is where parents can find the Homeschool Legal Defense Association and legal advice for every state in the union.
- KhanAcademy.org is where our kids are learning math at their own pace for free!
- Edragogy.com is a homeschool-friendly place to earn dual-enrollment credits for a good price.
- Tumblebooks.com is an awesome animated reading site where kids can learn to read along with the audio. It can be free if your library allows you access to it.
- Visit Troy.edu and ask about their accelerated program to see if your high school student can earn online dual-enrollment credit.
- ICR.org is a website of the Institute for Creation Research, where you can start by requesting their free magazine. The site offers lots of scientifically proven facts and resources.
- NHERI.org is the home of the National Home Education Research Institute, where you can send the naysayers who need to see the statistics that show that homeschooling works.
- TabletClass.com is a good place to learn math.

Influential Books

- The Bible—all of it, especially Deuteronomy 6 and the book of Proverbs.
- Mary Pride's two books, *The Way Home* and *All the Way Home*. These books taught me of the dangers of feminism and the joy and freedom of being a stay-at-home mom.

- *How to Teach Your Child to Read in 100 Easy Lessons* by Siegfried Engelmann, Phyllis Haddox, and Elaine Bruner. Once your child can get through this they are reading at the second-grade level.
- *A Full Quiver* by Rick and Jan Hess. This is basically why we have ten kids and are praying for more.
- *No Regrets: How Homeschooling Earned Me a Master's Degree at Age Sixteen* by Alexandra Swann. My first look into starting college early.
- *A Mom Just Like You* by Vickie Farris. This mom gave me the confidence to write.
- *Better Late Than Early* by Raymond and Dorothy Moore. This book helped me to relax in some areas.
- *Cheaper by the Dozen* by Ernestine Gilbreth Carey, with her brother Frank B. Gilbreth Jr. I read the original version of the book back in the fifth grade and thought about how fun it would be to live in a large family like theirs.
- *Belles on Their Toes* by Ernestine Gilbreth Carey and Frank B. Gilbreth Jr.
- *I Kissed Dating Goodbye* by Joshua Harris is great for every young person to read.
- *To Train Up a Child* by Michael and Debi Pearl. A bit legalistic.
- *Created to Be His Help Meet* by Debi Pearl. Every engaged or married woman should read this book.
- Any good biography of Susanna Wesley will help moms everywhere to keep things in perspective. This woman went through a lot while raising her large family.
- *Be Fruitful and Multiply* by Nancy Campbell. Speaks for itself.
- *Hard Times in Paradise* and *Homeschooling for Excellence* by David and Micki Colfax. Their homesteading story shows how kids learn by doing.

- *The Duggars: 20 and Counting!* and *A Love That Multiplies* by Jim Bob and Michelle Duggar. She homeschools and has nineteen kids now. Wow, what an inspiration.
- *Up from Slavery* by Booker T. Washington. This man exemplified what it means to do your best in all that you do, even in the little things.
- *Confessions of a Medical Heretic* by Robert S. Mendelsohn. We appreciate the advances of modern medicine but this book, though a little extreme, will give you a healthy, balanced view so that you can make informed choices for your kids' health.
- *Going Rogue: An American Life* by Sarah Palin. This book will teach you and your kids a lot about politics and the election process.

Influential People

- A student in Dr. Chan's University of Phoenix class who had the nerve to say, "Children in big families have low IQs." (Ouch! We took this as a challenge.)
- The homeschooling night-shift nurse I discussed earlier. She showed me that it really can be done with hard work.
- Tracy, a great friend who gave me *A Full Quiver* by Rick and Jan Hess. It gave me the peace to trust in the Lord for our family size. Now I love to give this book away so that others can find peace, too.
- Cafi Cohen, the author of the book *And What About College?*, was at a homeschool conference speaking about transcripts. She showed me that all of life's experiences can be educational

and how to put together a transcript. I also learned about child-led learning in her book (a concept that Kip always believed in).

- A fifteen-year-old girl who shared her story at a convention. I learned about the California High School Proficiency Exam (CHSPE) at that homeschooling conference.

Movies and Music

- The movie found at IndoctriNationMovie.com will turn some people off public education. It is a documentary film that explores the origins of the American education system.
- Play any music by Jamie Grace to get your kids out of bed and hoppin' as they do their chores.
- The movie *Dragons or Dinosaurs?* can be found at DragonsFilm .com.
- *Monumental* at MonumentalMovie.com. Kirk Cameron has a true following among homeschoolers. He is a man of God blessing our generation and the generations to come.
- *Demographic Winter* is a documentary that will teach your kids the truth about population growth.
- Louie Giglio, "Laminin" (short version), at www.youtube.com/ watch?v=F0-NPPIeeRk. This is an interesting perspective on how the human body is held together.
- *Pride and Prejudice* starring Keira Knightley. Great movie for learning proper diction/social studies/history. Kip's favorite line as a dad: "I'm quite at my leisure."—Donald Sutherland.

The Brainy Bunch Dance Party List

ARTIST/BAND	SONG
Beckah Shae	Incorruptible
Beckah Shae	Supernova
Big Daddy Weave	Redeemed [slow dance]
Britt Nicole	Gold
Britt Nicole (featuring Lecrae)	Ready or Not
Capital Kings	All the Way
Cupid	Cupid Shuffle
Diana Ross	I'm Coming Out
DJ Casper	Cha Cha Slide
Enrique Iglesias	Escape
Group 1 Crew	Manipulation
Group 1 Crew	Wait
Group 1 Crew	Let It Roll
Jamie Grace	Hold Me
Jamie Grace	God Girl
Jamie Grace	Show Jesus
Je'kob	Don't Let Go
Joann Rosario	Open My Eyes Lord
Kenny Loggins	Footloose
Kirk Franklin	I Smile
Kirk Franklin	Stomp
Lynyrd Skynyrd	Sweet Home Alabama

Mandisa	Good Morning
Mary Mary	God in Me
Mary Mary	Shackles
Needtobreathe	Washed by the Water [slow dance]
Newsboys	Something Beautiful
Owl City	Galaxies
Plumb	In My Arms
Press Play	#LITO
Rachael Lampa	Remedy
Rebecca St. James	Breathe [slow dance]
Stacie Orrico	Stuck
Supremes	You Can't Hurry Love
ZOEgirl	Mix of Life

Here is an alphabetized list of movies we really like and recommend as showing positive educational value:

101 Dalmatians
Aladdin
Bambi
Beauty and the Beast
Brave
Cars
Chitty Chitty Bang Bang
Cinderella
Cloudy with a Chance of Meatballs
Finding Nemo

The Jungle Book
Lady and the Tramp
The Lion King
Mary Poppins
Mulan
Old Yeller
Peter Pan
Pocahontas
Pollyanna
Robin Hood
Sleeping Beauty
Snow White and the Seven Dwarfs
Swiss Family Robinson
Tangled
Tarzan
The Fox and the Hound
The Little Mermaid
The Sound of Music
Twenty Thousand Leagues Under the Sea
Up
WALL-E

Educational Books Worth Reading

There is a really funny book titled *Teaching Old Logs New Tricks: More Absurdities and Realities of Education*. The cartoons are by Michael F. Giangreco and illustrations by Kevin Ruelle. They deal with very serious subjects in a lighthearted way. They really get teachers to think about their profession and remind homeschoolers of the realities of traditional education. This book should be reviewed by every school in America and some questions should be asked about the status quo.

Another great book is *How to Write an IEP, 3rd Edition* by John Arena. ("IEP" stands for "individualized education program.") If you have a special needs child, see how the professional educators do it. Page 93 lists fully inclusive goals and calls for "chronologically age-appropriate general education classrooms in their normal school of attendance." That is so your child doesn't just get labeled, segregated, and effectively left behind. And this is a good thing, but don't settle for that minimum standard. Your challenged child still possesses God-imparted beautiful uniqueness that only you can nurture to maturity as the parent. You have even more reason to tailor your child's education toward their unique gift(s)—never settle, never retreat from believing in them, and love them to the fullest.

The inclusiveness goals also suggest that these special needs students should move with peers to subsequent grades in school. This is also good so they get exposed to more knowledge, but don't let them suffer the full brunt of a standardized curriculum. Let them shine in the light of day. Let your children see the two of you in the mirror cheek to cheek, knowing that you are a team together. Let no one and nothing come between you and assure them that all their successes and failures in life will be shared or endured together.

In the book *Tyranny Through Public Education: The Case Against Government Control of Education* by William F. Cox, page 541 states, "Parents are still branded as suspiciously unable to rear their own children from those who self-promote that they know best how to teach children." Don't believe it in the aggregate. In other words, most of what you already know is good enough for your little ones.

You can teach your child the elementary subjects and you are a good judge of whether they are learning up to a certain level. When you reach the limits of your own knowledge, seek out extra help. Even if English is not your first language or theirs, you can learn together! Speaking of which, for those who like to do research, a compilation of writings that may interest you is the book *Teaching the Chinese Learner: Psychological and Pedagogical Perspectives* by David Watkins and John Biggs. Page 199 states, interestingly, "Even though constructivist instruction did not boost conventional test scores, these teachers gradually shifted from a quantitative towards a more qualitative view of teaching and learning." Meaning-making is something all students may try to achieve out of educational material, but enlightening them with the love of God builds trust and assures them they are more valued than any test score, good or bad.

It is great for parents to read materials such as those above, but the best reading of all is that done with your child in the Word of God.

Websites We Like

Kip
- My website for ski info, slopedope.com.

Mona Lisa
- ChristianAnswers.net has great movie reviews.
- There's a nice transcript template at www.hslda.org/highschool/academics.asp#TR.
- Scholastic.com: click on the "Kids" tab to find books of the right age for your kids.

- Mardel.com: This website offers Bibles, books, music, arts and crafts supplies, and jewelry. They have a special homeschool area with tips and lesson ideas.

Heath

A passion I have is the digital currency sector. I have purchased a few domains that I hope to use for businesses catering to holders of the currency called bitcoin (and others like Novacoin), including The-CoinUpdate.com and TradeforBitcoin.com. I'm going to go out on a limb and say that, Lord willing, I will have built complete websites at these domains before this book's release.

Others I like:

- JonesGeniuses.com has accelerated math and reading curricula for sale.
- Gutenberg.org has public domain books available for free download.
- Wikipedia.org and Wikibooks.org have tons of high-quality information.

Keith

- Teoria.com for music theory and ear training.
- MuseScore.org hosts fantastic free software for music typesetting.

Seth

- Hurstwic.org has some interesting historical information on Vikings.

- Video of us on Fox and Friends: foxnewsinsider.com/2013/05/24/harding-family-sends-6-kids-college-age-12
- This link is good for other kids to see our kids. I have had peo-

ple tell us that their kids were really inspired by our kids and can see themselves doing the same thing: www.today.com/news/meet-family-who-sent-six-kids-college-age-12-1C9316706#

- Collegeby12.com: This is our site where people can contact us for phone consultations and speaking engagements.

Appendix B: Sample Transcripts

Student: Church Cover School:
20XX-20XX School Year   XXXXX
SSN: XXX-XX-XXXX   PO Box XXXX
                                                                    City, State Zip

Year Taken	Subject	Credits	Grade	Extra Curricular Activities
9th Grade	Bible	1		AYSO Soccer
	Pre-Algebra	1		Chess Club Member
	English 1 (Freshman Comp.)	1		
	General Science	1		
	Social Studies 1	0.5		
	Piano 1	0.5		
	Physical Education	0.5		
	Intro to Computer Applications	1		
		6.5		
10th Grade	Bible	1		Victory Sports League
	Algebra 1	1		Chess Club Member
	English 2 (Creative Writing)	1		AWANA
	Evolutionary/Creation Science	1		
	Beginning Violin	1		
	Physical Education	0.5		
	Choir	1		
		6.5		
11th Grade	Bible	1		AWANA
	Algebra 2	1		AYSO Soccer
	English 3 (Essay Writing)	1		
	Biology	1		
	Advanced Violin	0.5		
	US History	1		
	Physical Education	0.5		
	Music Appreciation	1		
		7.0		
12th Grade	Bible/ World History	1		AWANA
	Geometry	1		Part Time – Pet
	English 4 (College Prep.)	1		Sitting/ Animal Care
	Chemistry	1		
	Spanish 1	1		
	American Government	1		
	Physical Education -Tennis	0.5		
	Beginning Clarinet	0.5		Name First, Last
		7.0		High School Administrator
	Total Credits	**27.0**		←Current GPA

Graduation Date: _____

XXXXXX Academy Official Transcript

Student: Church Cover School:
Date of Birth: XXXXXX Academy
SSN: XXX-XX-XXXX   PO Box XXXX
                                          City, State Zip

Year Taken	Subject	Credits	Grade	Extra Curricular Activities
9th Grade	Bible	1		AYSO Soccer
	Pre-Algebra	1		Chess Club Member
	English 1 (Freshman Comp.)	1		AWANA
	General Science	1		
	Social Studies 1	0.5		
	World History	1		
	Physical Education	0.5		
	Art	0.5		
		6.5		
10th Grade	Bible	1		Victory Sports League
	Algebra 1	1		Chess Club Member
	English 2 (Creative Writing)	1		AWANA
	Evolutionary/Creation Science	1		
	Spanish 1	1		
	Physical Education	0.5		
	Geography	1		
		6.5		
11th Grade	Bible	1		AWANA
	Algebra 2	1		AYSO Soccer
	English 3 (Essay Writing)	1		
	Biology	1		
	Home Economics	0.5		
	US History	1		
	Physical Education	0.5		
	ACT Prep. Course	1		
		7.0		
12th Grade	Bible	1		AWANA
	Geometry	1		
	English 4 (College Prep.)	1		
	Economics	1		
	Anatomy & Physiology	1		
	American Government	1		ACT Score: XX
	Physical Education -Tennis	0.5		
	Beginning Trumpet	0.5		
		7.0		High School Administrator
	Total Credits	**27.0**		←Current GPA

Graduation Date: _____

Appendix C: Sample Kids' Schedule

Sunday

5 am			
6 am			
7 am			Dad Telecommute 7:00am–3:30pm
8 am			
9 am	Sunday School 9:00am–10:00am		
10 am		Church 10:15am–11:30am	
11 am			
12 pm			
1 pm			
2 pm	Ultimate Frisbee 2:00pm–4:00pm (Heath/Keith/Seth)		
3 pm			
4 pm		Church Outreach 3:45pm–5:00pm	
5 pm		K/M/L/T AWANA 5:30pm–7:00pm	
6 pm			
7 pm			Katie Rehearsal 7:00pm–10:00pm
8 pm			
9 pm			
10 pm			

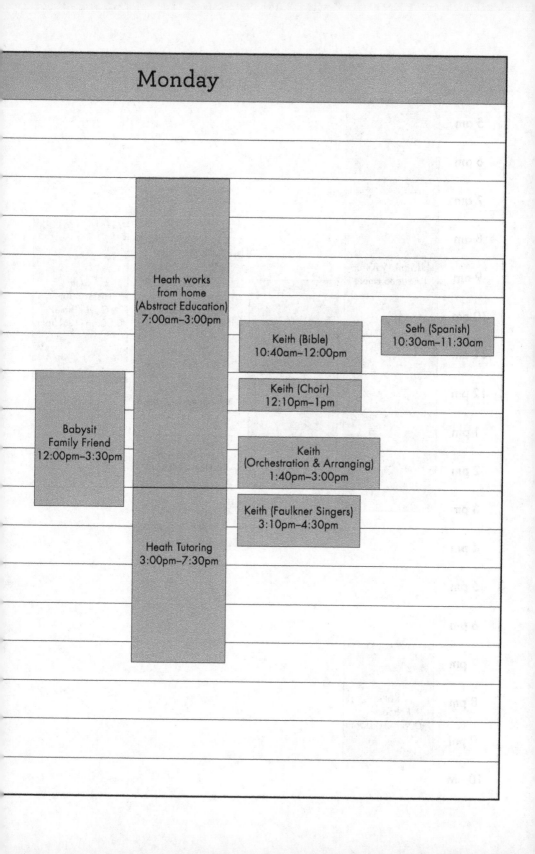

Monday

Heath works
from home
(Abstract Education)
7:00am–3:00pm

Keith (Bible)
10:40am–12:00pm

Seth (Spanish)
10:30am–11:30am

Keith (Choir)
12:10pm–1pm

Babysit
Family Friend
12:00pm–3:30pm

Keith
(Orchestration & Arranging)
1:40pm–3:00pm

Keith (Faulkner Singers)
3:10pm–4:30pm

Heath Tutoring
3:00pm–7:30pm

Tuesday

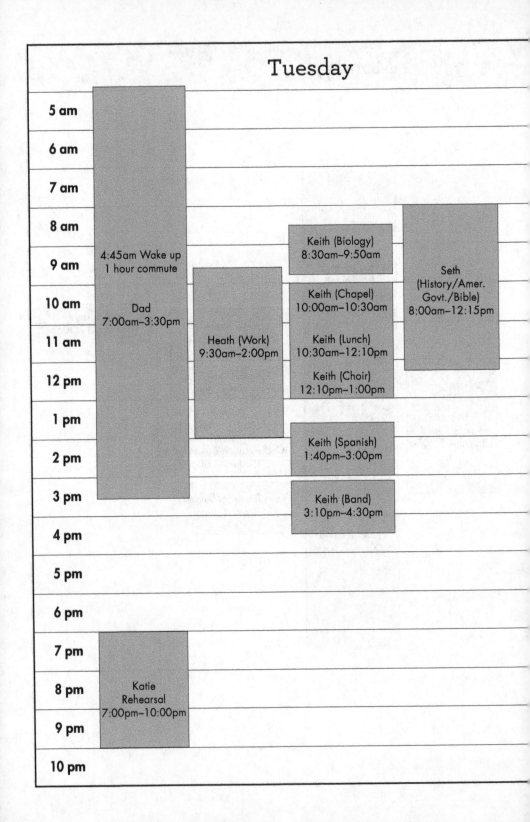

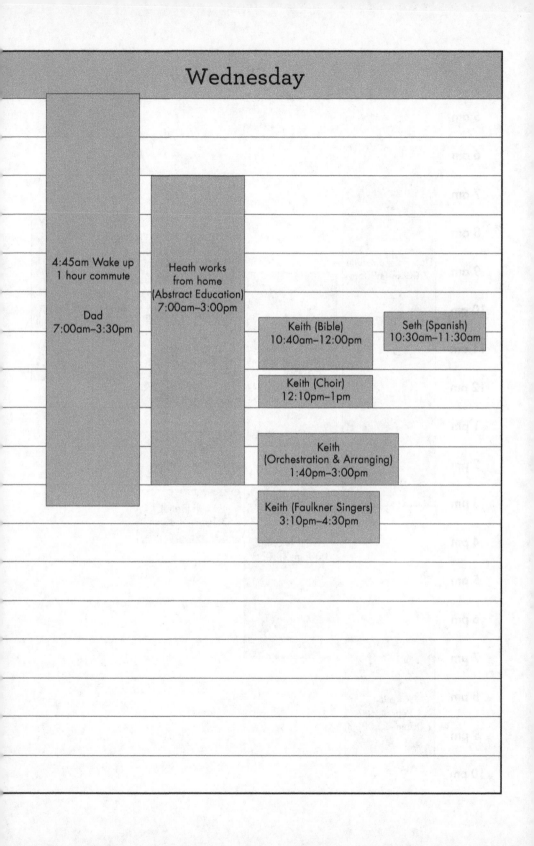

Thursday

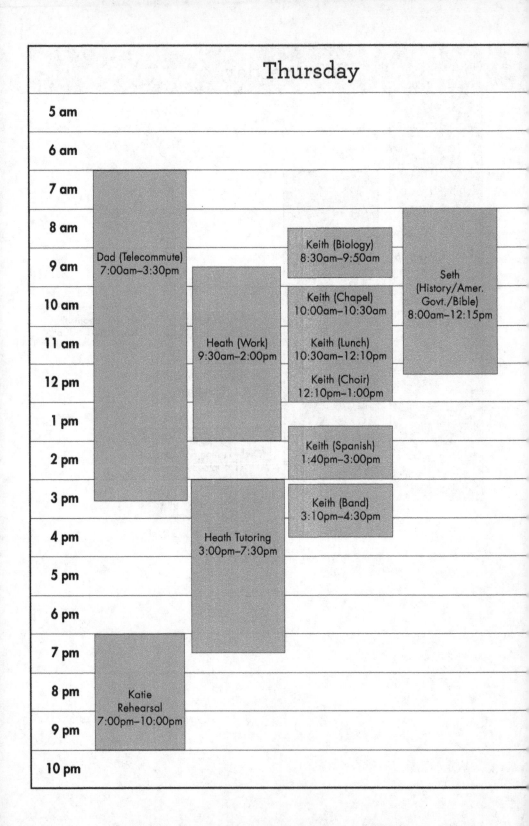

5 am			
6 am			
7 am	Dad (Telecommute) 7:00am–3:30pm		Seth (History/Amer. Govt./Bible) 8:00am–12:15pm
8 am		Keith (Biology) 8:30am–9:50am	
9 am	Heath (Work) 9:30am–2:00pm		
10 am		Keith (Chapel) 10:00am–10:30am	
11 am		Keith (Lunch) 10:30am–12:10pm	
12 pm		Keith (Choir) 12:10pm–1:00pm	
1 pm			
2 pm		Keith (Spanish) 1:40pm–3:00pm	
3 pm	Heath Tutoring 3:00pm–7:30pm	Keith (Band) 3:10pm–4:30pm	
4 pm			
5 pm			
6 pm			
7 pm	Katie Rehearsal 7:00pm–10:00pm		
8 pm			
9 pm			
10 pm			

Friday

5 am
6 am
7 am
8 am
9 am
12 pm
1 pm
2 pm
3 pm
4 pm
5 pm
6 pm
7 pm
8 pm
9 pm
10 pm

4:45am Wake up
1 hour commute

Dad
7:00am–3:30pm

Heath works
from home
(Abstract Education)
7:00am–3:00pm

Keith (Biology Lab)
10:40am–12:00pm

Seth (Spanish)
10:30am–11:30am

Keith
(Tutors Family Friend)
3:00pm–4:00pm

Katie
Rehearsal
7:00pm–10:00pm

Saturday

5 am	
6 am	
7 am	
8 am	
9 am	Heath works from home (Abstract Education) 7:00am–3:00pm
10 am	
11 am	
12 pm	
1 pm	
2 pm	
3 pm	
4 pm	
5 pm	
6 pm	
7 pm	
8 pm	
9 pm	
10 pm	

Disclaimer

The Harding family and College by 12 cannot guarantee the result that your child will start college by age 12. This book is for general guidance and inspiration only.

Consultations with the Hardings can be scheduled for help in answering further questions.

See www.collegeby12.com for consulting fees.

Acknowledgments

Kip would like to thank various agents for creating the opportunities to produce TV with us. Bob Dotson for NBC's *Today* show piece. CNN for naming us the "Brainy Bunch." Fox for keeping it real—all the time. Steve at Folio. Our editor, Natasha Simons, for all of her patience and hard work, our cowriter, Travis Thrasher, and everyone at Simon & Schuster for this publication.

To my father, Glyn O. Harding: Thank you for epitomizing the humble station of a father who knows best but shows the good grace to live and let live in so many matters of life.

To my mother, Grace W. Lawrence: May god grant you the fullness of your faith in all that you have and do believe.

Mona Lisa: Thanks to Nicki at *People*, Steve & Wesa, Connie and Gary, and Keith & Penny.

To my mom, for being both mom and dad during those crucial early years.

Heath would like to thank all his classmates who created such a positive college experience for him.

Serennah: I would like to acknowledge my family—all of them—extended and close. And anyone I have ever called friend. Because of each of you, my life has been fun living, and hopefully for you—fun to watch.